THERE'S NO STANDING STILL

How to Grow a Profitable Dental Practice Focusing on You, Your People and Your Patients

Personal Action Guide

DR. SEAN MOHTASHAMI

SPOTLIGHT
PUBLISHING HOUSE

Goodyear, Arizona

There's No Standing Still – How to Grow a Profitable Dental Practice Focusing on You, Your People, and Your Patients.

ISBN: 978-1-962570-21-3

Interior Design: Marigold2k
Contributing Authors: Julieanne O'Connor, Steve Sperry,
Steven Rowell
Published By: Spotlight Publishing House https://spotlightpublishinghouse.com

Introduction

This Personal Action Guide contains all of the tools, checklists, and scripts listed at the end of each chapter of the book. I hope you will find great value in utilizing these resources on your own and with your teams.

This guide is organized in the order of the book chapters for easy reference. Any duplication of tools in more than one chapter is for your convenience. You may also find these resources available online via www.TheresNoStandingStill.com

I'd love to hear from you with any thoughts, insights, suggestions, or celebrations you may have after working with these tools. Please share your thoughts with me on the book website. I enjoy reading your comments and appreciate you investing your time to improve yourself, your people, and your practice so you can deliver excellent patient care.

There's No Standing Still in the Pursuit of Excellence!

—Dr. Sean

You

CHAPTER 1

Building Blocks for Personal Success

The Quality of Life 100 Self-Assessment

Instructions:

1. Check the box if the statement is consistently true for you.
2. If the statement does not apply to you, please change the language so that it does, or replace it with a different statement that fits within the category, then evaluate the new statement is consistently true for you.
3. Add up your section scores and your Total score.
4. Check back every 30 or 90 days and you will likely see progress, even if you aren't focusing directly on this.
5. Work with a coach to help you get through the challenging times.

1. Family & Relationships

- ☐ 1. I am pleased/content with my spouse/partner, or happy being single.
- ☐ 2. I am close to my parents, alive or not. There is nothing in the way, or between us.
- ☐ 3. I have a circle of friends who I enjoy, without any effort.
- ☐ 4. I have a best friend and treat him/her extremely well.
- ☐ 5. I am close to my children. There is nothing in the way.
- ☐ 6. I enjoy my family/extended family; we have worked through any dysfunction and past problems.
- ☐ 7. I am part of a professional network that stimulates me intellectually and emotionally.
- ☐ 8. I get along well with my neighbors.
- ☐ 9. I have at least 10 friends and colleagues who live outside of my city of residence.
- ☐ 10.I am loved by the people who mean the most to me.

______ Section Score (Number of checked boxes)

2. Career & Business

- ☐ 11. My work/career is both fulfilling and nourishing to me; I am not drained.
- ☐ 12. I am highly regarded for my expertise by my Patients, team members, & colleagues.
- ☐ 13. I am on a positive career path leading to opportunities and increased income.

- ☐ 14. I work in the right industry or field; it has a bright future.
- ☐ 15. I look forward to going to work virtually every day.
- ☐ 16. My work is not my life, but it is a rich part of my life.
- ☐ 17. I work with the right people.
- ☐ 18. My work environment brings out the very best of me because it is wonderfully stimulating and/or very supportive.
- ☐ 19. At the end of the day, I have as much energy as I did when I started the day, I am not drained.
- ☐ 20. The work I do helps to meet my intellectual, social and/or emotional needs.

______ Section Score (Number of checked boxes)

3. Money & Finances

- ☐ 21. I have at least a year's living expenses in the bank or money market fund.
- ☐ 22. I am on a financial independence track or I am already there.
- ☐ 23. I don't have to work at financial success; money seems to find me with little effort.
- ☐ 24. I have no financial stress of any kind in my life.
- ☐ 25. I invest at least 10% of my income/earnings in my ability to increase my income.
- ☐ 26. I do not carry credit card debt; I do not overspend.
- ☐ 27. When I buy something, I buy the best possible quality.
- ☐ 28. I don't lose sleep over my investments.
- ☐ 29. I am financially knowledgeable—I know how money is made and lost.
- ☐ 30. I make money because I provide more than enough value to the people/customers who need what I have.

______ Section Score (Number of checked boxes)

4. Joy & Delight

- ☐ 31. I spend my leisure time totally enjoying my interests; I am never bored.
- ☐ 32. Weekends (or other days off) are a joy for me.
- ☐ 33. I have designed the perfect way to spend the last hour of my day.
- ☐ 34. I look forward to getting up virtually every morning.
- ☐ 35. I am happy.
- ☐ 36. I have designed—and I am living—the perfect lifestyle for me right now.
- ☐ 37. I have at least an hour a day that is exclusively for me; I spend it in a chosen way.
- ☐ 38. I can stay present during the day; I don't lose myself to stress.
- ☐ 39. I easily take delight in the smallest things.
- ☐ 40. My home brings me joy every time I walk inside.

______ Section Score (Number of checked boxes)

5. Effectiveness & Efficiency

- ☐ 41. I don't spend time with anyone who bugs me or who is using me.
- ☐ 42. I have more than enough energy/vitality to get through the day without dragging.
- ☐ 43. I have no problem asking for exactly what I want, from anyone.
- ☐ 44. I have all the right tools, equipment, computers, software and peripherals that I need to work well.
- ☐ 45. Whatever can be automated, is automated.
- ☐ 46. Whatever can be delegated, is delegated.
- ☐ 47. I reply to all emails as I read them; I don't maintain inbox of unanswered emails.
- ☐ 48. I don't put things off; when it occurs to me, I do it, handle it or have it done.
- ☐ 49. I know what my goals are, and I am eagerly/effectively making them real.
- ☐ 50. I don't do errands, except by exception.

______ Section Score (Number of checked boxes)

6. Responsibility & Foundation

- ☐ 51. I love my home: Its location, style, furnishings, light and feeling.
- ☐ 52. My boundaries are strong enough that people respect me, my needs and what I want.
- ☐ 53. I tolerate little; I'm just not willing to.
- ☐ 54. I don't see a cloud on my future's horizon; it looks clear.
- ☐ 55. My wants have been satisfied; there is little I want.
- ☐ 56. My personal needs have been satisfied; I am not driven or motivated by unmet needs.
- ☐ 57. There is nothing I am dreading or avoiding.
- ☐ 58. My personal values are clear; I am oriented around them.
- ☐ 59. I have resolved the stresses and key issues of my upbringing and past events.
- ☐ 60. I don't have a lot of unfinished projects, business or hanging items; I am caught up.

______ Section Score (Number of checked boxes)

7. Personal Development & Evolution

- ☐ 61. I could die this afternoon with no regrets.
- ☐ 62. I am living my life, not the life that someone else designed for me or expected of me.
- ☐ 63. There is nothing that I am not facing head-on; nothing I am putting off dealing with.
- ☐ 64. I attract success; I don't have to strive for it or chase it.
- ☐ 65. I have more than enough natural motivation, inspiration and synergy in my life, I am not stuck.
- ☐ 66. I am evolving, not just improving, because I continually experiment.
- ☐ 67. I have progressed beyond the notion of beliefs.
- ☐ 68. I am at that place in life where I initiate and cause events, not wait for others or events to do so.
- ☐ 69. I have learned to take the path of least resistance as I accomplish my goals.
- ☐ 70. I am beyond striving for success; I simply enjoy life and focus on what fulfills me.

______ Section Score (Number of checked boxes)

8. Self-Care & Vitality

- ☐ 71. I take at least 3 vacations per year.
- ☐ 72. Life is easy; I have virtually no problems or unresolved matters affecting me.
- ☐ 73. My teeth and gums look great and are in top condition.
- ☐ 74. I have more than enough time during my day.
- ☐ 75. I eat food for sustenance and pleasure, not for emotional comfort.
- ☐ 76. I am not abusing my body with too much alcohol, television, caffeine, food, drugs or any other addictive substances or behaviors.
- ☐ 77. Whatever health problems I have, I am receiving proper, effective care for them.
- ☐ 78. My body is in great shape.
- ☐ 79. I reduce stress daily by meditating, taking a long bath, exercising, walking, etc.
- ☐ 80. There is nothing I am doing that is messing up my mind or heart.

______ Section Score (Number of checked boxes)

9. Happiness & Contentment

Please write down 10 situations, routines or scenarios that make, or would make, you the happiest and most content.

- ☐ 81. ______________________________
- ☐ 82. ______________________________
- ☐ 83. ______________________________
- ☐ 84. ______________________________
- ☐ 85. ______________________________
- ☐ 86. ______________________________
- ☐ 87. ______________________________
- ☐ 88. ______________________________
- ☐ 89. ______________________________
- ☐ 90. ______________________________

Now re-read the list and check the boxes of those that exist for you now.

______ Section Score (Number of checked boxes)

10. Pleasure & Excitement

Please write down 10 activities that you truly enjoy, whether you currently do these things in your life or not.

- ☐ 91. ______
- ☐ 92. ______
- ☐ 93. ______
- ☐ 94. ______
- ☐ 95. ______
- ☐ 96. ______
- ☐ 97. ______
- ☐ 98. ______
- ☐ 99. ______
- ☐ 100. ______

Now re-read the list and check the boxes of those that exist for you now.

______ Section Score (Number of checked boxes)

TOTAL SCORE (Total of all Section Scores—100 is highest possible)

Scoring Key:

90-100 Congratulations. Incredible. You have much to celebrate.
80-89 Excellent! Your score is very high—this is a tough test.
70-79 Very good. You're on track. Keep going.
60-69 Pretty good, but there is some work to do. Average Score. Perhaps prioritize your quality of life-score 10 more points in the next month?
40-49 You may need to make some important changes. Perhaps enroll a Coach, Counselor or Support Person
30-39 OK. Acknowledge and then seek support for yourself. You deserve it!
00-29 This may be painful and feel overwhelming...you are not alone. Seek support from those you trust.

10 Steps to a Strong Personal Foundation

1. Honor your boundaries.
   Boundaries protect you from people that your spirit cannot easily afford.

2. Raise your standards.
   The higher your standards, the fewer problems you will experience in life.

3. Clarify your requirements.
   Everyone in your life deserves to know what you expect/require of them.

4. Finish your unfinished business.
   The fewer unresolved items in your life, the more confident you will feel.

5. Get your personal needs met.
   Until your personal needs are met, it's difficult to live powerfully and sustainably.

6. Orient around your values.
   When you orient your life and your goals around your values, fulfillment naturally occurs.

7. Build reserves in all areas.
   Having more than enough calms the mind and affords more experimentation in life.

8. Identify and reduce tolerations.
   What you put up with drains your energy and slows your development.

9. Handle the money, completely.
   Until your money is handled, you are not at choice in life.

10. Define success for yourself.
    When you define success for yourself, life becomes very, very simple.

Energy Drains Exercise

What are you tolerating/putting up with that drains your energy?

We put up with, accept, take on and are dragged down by people's behavior, situations, unmet needs, crossed boundaries, in-completions, problems and even our own behavior (avoidance, silence, compliance). You are putting up with more than you may think, so what are you tolerating in your life, right now. Be specific.

Examples:

1. My living arrangements
2. Lack of storage space at home
3. Unorganized/Unusable Garage at home
4. My weight
5. My job not being satisfying, rewarding or challenging anymore
6. Financial worries
7. Too much spending on luxury items
8. Foot pain that I keep avoiding/not dealing with
9. Self-doubt about my….
10. Procrastinating on completing my taxes
11. Not cleaning up the backyard storage shed
12. Not dealing with car repairs
13. Credit card debt out of control
14. Arguing with my spouse
15. Worrying about the future rather than focusing on the present
16. Messy office workspace
17. Too many emails stored without responding to them
18. Too much unresolved mail at home
19. Dirty laundry in the back bathroom (avoiding)
20. Disappointment about no longer attending church
21. Going out too many evenings each week with friends
22. Not enough sleep
23. Not exercising
24. Unresolved anger with….
25. Not dealing directly with….

Energy Drains Exercise

Make a list of at least 20 things that you are tolerating in your life.

Then, reflecting on your list, consider the following:

What are you willing to do to change?

What is not addressing these items costing you right now?

Your Opportunity: Identify the first 5 of these tolerations you will eliminate, or at least decrease/change the impact of them, within the next 30 days.

For each item you are eliminating, you get to come up with a list of what you will **STOP doing** to eliminate this item, and **START doing,** and **CONTINUE doing.**

1. ______________________________
2. ______________________________
3. ______________________________
4. ______________________________
5. ______________________________
6. ______________________________
7. ______________________________
8. ______________________________
9. ______________________________
10. ______________________________
11. ______________________________
12. ______________________________
13. ______________________________
14. ______________________________
15. ______________________________
16. ______________________________
17. ______________________________
18. ______________________________
19. ______________________________
20. ______________________________

CHAPTER 2

Striving for Excellence: Unleash Your Full Potential

Stop, Start, Continue Feedback Exercise

Two of the more powerful and effective tools I share with my clients for them to use in facilitating team meetings and individual meetings as well are, Stop, Start, Continue and Mad, Glad and Sad.

Some of the most common situations to use these tools in are:

- Teambuilding with staff or management teams
- Soliciting feedback from front-line staff
- Facilitating constructive coaching conversations with an individual
- Discussions with almost anyone when your need is to discover the "real issues" of a situation or a relationship

Stop, Start, Continue and Mad, Glad and Sad can be completed in private by groups of individuals, in dialogue with an individual, or as an interactive team exercise for an entire team simultaneously (using flipcharts for data capture).

A traditional example of using Stop, Start, Continue with a group of employees, is to pass one copy of the Stop, Start, Continue form to each participant. Then ask everyone to quietly, with no discussion, read through the handout and then ask them to write down their responses to the following questions privately using the Stop, Start, Continue handout.

You could then facilitate a group discussion, asking individual participants to share whatever they are comfortable sharing in discussion with the entire group.

This Stop, Start, Continue form can be used with individuals in private one-on-one conversations as well in an effort to offer a tool to guide your discussion. You could send the form to the person in advance of your meeting as well if this makes your face-to-face time more meaningful and efficient.

Another method of using this Stop, Start, Continue process is to bring a group of 10-12 employees or managers together (traditionally this is not used with managers and staff in the same group—at least in the beginning of your use of this process). Using flipcharts around the room, one labeled STOP, one labeled START and one labeled CONTINUE, you simply ask everyone to either approach the flip chart pages and write their ideas down under each category, or use post it notes first—with one idea written per post-it, and then ask the participants to place their post-its on the flipchart pages under each category.

There are advantages and disadvantages to each of these data collection methods for Stop, Start, Continue (or Mad, Glad and Sad).

Method One—asking participants to use markers and write their ideas under each Category, STOP, START, CONTINUE.

ADVANTAGES:

- Participants are able to move around the room at their own will
- Participants are able to write down their own thoughts without having to share with the larger group
- Data collection tends to be extremely fast due to the fact that people disburse throughout the room—this is especially true for larger groups when you post multiple blank flipchart pages on the walls for each category, STOP, START, CONTINUE
- Flipchart pages can be easily stored for use later in typing up the data from the meeting

DISADVANTAGES:

- Participants tend to watch people as they write their comments down on the flipchart pages which can prove challenging or anxiety provoking for some participants—this contributes to the possibility for group think to occur as well—that is, participants to change their responses after seeing what others have begun to write on the various flipcharts—to an extreme, participants becoming biased by the presence of one or two comments and then these participants simply following along with these few statements rather than contributing what they are truly feeling or needing to express.

Method Two—asking participants to use POST-IT Notes, one post-it per idea, and then participants place each of their POST-IT Notes under each Category, STOP, START, CONTINUE.

ADVANTAGES:

- Participants perceive greater privacy, because they fill out each POST-IT note in the room with the group, but without letting anyone see what they are writing
- Participants get out of their seats to place their POST-IT notes, but again, most participants cannot see what is written on other people's POST-IT notes during this process
- The use of POST-IT notes allows you or the facilitator to organize the POST- IT notes quickly under each category in themes, or to consolidate repetitious comments
- Repetitious comments can be easily organized by placing POST-IT notes together in a line for each category, which visually shows the frequency of comments for each theme under each category. Some of my clients put the POST-IT notes in columns or rows in order to show the frequencies of each issues, resulting in a bar graph of POST-IT notes or a histogram.

DISADVANTAGES:

- Once the POST-IT notes are put on the flipchart pages, they are difficult to be read by participants once everyone is back in their seats for discussion— the handwriting tends to be small.
- After the meeting, the handling of the flipchart pages is a little more tedious because the POST-IT notes can tend to fall off or move as the flipchart pages are folded and utilized later

Once your team's data is collected, you can use a variety of methods to have your team prioritize the various themes or ideas under each category, STOP, START and CONTINUE.

A similar process is used to solicit feedback using Mad, Glad and Sad. The best method is to conduct Mad, Glad and Sad exercise first. Then conduct the *Stop, Start, Continue* exercise.

Examples of questions to use in the use of Stop, Start, Continue are:

- What could we Stop, Start or Continue to do together as a department, to make this a better place to work?
- What could I Stop, Start or Continue to do as your boss, to become an even better boss?
- What do each of us need to Stop, Start or Continue doing in order to become more effective team members?
- Thinking of the way in which this team communicates on a regular basis, what do we need to Stop, Start or Continue doing?

Examples of questions to use in the use of Mad, Glad and Sad are:

- Thinking of your daily work life here at work, what are you Mad about, Glad about, and Sad about?
- When you think of how our team interacts and supports each other, what are you Mad about, Glad about and Sad about?
- When you think of how we treat our customers or patients, what are you Mad about, Glad about and Sad about?
- The only "rules" to use when soliciting feedback from participants using these two tools:
- If you provide an idea under one category, please offer another idea under one of the other categories—e.g., if you list a Stop, list a Start too; if you list a Mad, list a Glad too.
- Your contribution must be genuine, constructive and sensitively worded.

Confidential Version

If confidentiality is critically important (especially the first time you conduct this feedback exercise) you may prefer to use this confidential method of collecting participants' feedback data.

Provide everyone a single piece of 8.5 x 11 paper, a pen, and an "interoffice-type envelope." For both Mad, Glad and Sad, and Stop, Start and Continue, ask each participant to privately write down their thoughts under each category, e.g., Mad, Glad, Sad, on one side of the paper. Then use the other side of the paper for Stop, Start, Continue. Once each participant is finished, they may put their own paper, and only their paper, into their envelope. Then they simply pass their closed envelopes forward.

Using this method, typically the data is collected in the envelopes, and the data is compiled confidentially and then reported back to all participants.

Examples of How to Frame the Questions

The following examples simply demonstrate how to ask the questions as they related to a specific topic or issue.

These feedback exercises are routinely used to solicit feedback from team members in the following areas:

- Teamwork and communication between departments and/or team members
- Improving the Patient experience
- Increasing Accountability amongst the team
- Leaders asking for feedback about how they can better support their team
- Improving processes, systems or methods within the business, e.g., ordering supplies; following up with former Patients
- Improving safety procedures, policies and practices
- Identifying cost savings or ways to sell more services and/or products

Obviously, you may have other topics as well.

Here is an example of how to modify the questions to fit each topic:

"When you think about the past 6 months, and how we have been ordering supplies, what are you Mad about, Sad about and Glad about?"

Then conduct the Stop, Start and Continue version using this question.

"Thinking of the current Patient experience we provide our Patients, what are you Mad, Glad and Sad about?" Then, Stop, Start and Continue.

"When you think about teamwork, communication amongst team members/departments, and accountability, what are you Mad, Sad and Glad about?"

You can do each item separately if you wish, e.g., teamwork and they write down their thoughts; then you ask about communication, and they write; and then you ask about accountability. This usually creates clearer data in terms of their comments and connecting them with the correct topic.

- What am I GLAD about?

- What are my priorities to address?

- What Should We START doing?

- What Should We CONTINUE doing?

- What are the BENEFITS to us, our Patients, and others?

CURRENT CONCERNS:

What am I MAD about?

What am I SAD about?

What am I GLAD about?

What are my priorities to address?

PERSONAL COMMITMENTS:

What Should I STOP doing?

What Should I START doing?

What Should I CONTINUE doing?

What are the BENEFITS to me?

Co-Creating Behavior Standards Checklist

Tips for Designing and Implementing Behavior Standards:

- ☐ They are also referred to as Standards of Performance, Performance Standards or Standards in Practice.
- ☐ Become crystal clear about what your vision is for implementing these standards, what you are trying to accomplish, and why you are doing it.
- ☐ Seek input from all employees in creating the document. This takes time but is the most valuable aspect of the process for ensuring employee buy-in later which is priceless.
- ☐ Align desired behaviors with organizational goals and desired outcomes—make sure the priorities match and ring true.
- ☐ Review other organizations' Standards of Behavior—study the successful implementations of others.
- ☐ Be crystal clear and very specific in your wording. Say exactly what you mean and avoid colloquialisms and jargon. For instance, state, "make eye contact, smile and verbally greet all guests who come within five feet of you at any time."
- ☐ Hold a ceremonial Standards of Behavior "roll out." Have all existing employees sign their commitment to the new Standards.
- ☐ Hold people accountable when they violate a standard. Model the importance of these standards consistently and endlessly, by senior and middle management.
- ☐ Create a designated "Standard of the Month." Post and distribute liberally throughout the organization for the first 12 months after initial introduction.
- ☐ Update the Standards of Behavior over time to keep them current.
- ☐ Have new applicants sign it right up front—preview it on your website and job application, review it in the interview process and then have the new hire sign their commitment on their first day of orientation to the company.
- ☐ Keep your list of Standards to no more than 7 with brief, clear descriptions of the behavior expected for this standard.

Sample Behavioral Standards

Respect
- Patients First is our Focus
- Respect and honor our employees and physicians
- Model mutual respect by caregivers and leaders

Privacy and Confidentiality
- Maintain confidentiality of patient information at all times
- Respect the privacy needs of our patients
- Conduct appropriate conversations at all times

Quality
- Provide exceptional clinical care to every patient we serve
- Fully embrace the patient's Right To Know
- Demonstrate commitment to continuous improvement

Professionalism
- Serve as a role model of Company at all times
- Choose your attitude daily, with Patients and Guests in mind
- Look and act the part of a health care professional always

Safety
- Provide a clean, healthy and safe environment
- Work smarter, think Safety first

Communication
- Fully explain care procedures to our patients in advance
- Be sensitive to the individual needs of our patients
- Keep patients informed about their care throughout their stay
- Listen to and share information in a timely manner between co-workers

Teamwork
- Provide exceptional responsiveness from our staff
- All share in the commitment to co-workers for effective teamwork
- Support the goals of the organization

Accountability
- Everyone takes pride in the work we do and the services we provide
- Each of us holds ourselves accountable in providing exceptional care to our patients
- Each team member is accountable for their own choices

How to Build a High-Performance Culture Checklist

- ☐ Capture Incoming Calls, Texts, Emails and Chat
- ☐ Conversion to Appointments
- ☐ Show Up Rate
- ☐ Diagnosing All Treatments
- ☐ Treatment Conversations
- ☐ Pre-Payment
- ☐ Treatment Efficiency
- ☐ Follow-up Appointments
- ☐ Post-Treatment Follow-up
- ☐ Hire the Right People
- ☐ Create a Positive Work Environment
- ☐ Set Clear Goals
- ☐ Provide Ongoing Training & Development
- ☐ Recognize Achievements
- ☐ Encourage Collaboration & Teamwork
- ☐ Foster Open Communication
- ☐ Offer Flexible Scheduling
- ☐ Measure Performance
- ☐ Celebrate Successes/Reinforce Positive Behaviors
- ☐ Provide Feedback

CHAPTER 3

The Wheel of Life: Balancing the Important Areas of Your Life

The Wheel of Life Personal Map

Focus on "The Big 5"

I decided to narrow down my wheel to focus on five areas of my life, which when done well, have a significant impact on my results, my experiences, and my relationships.

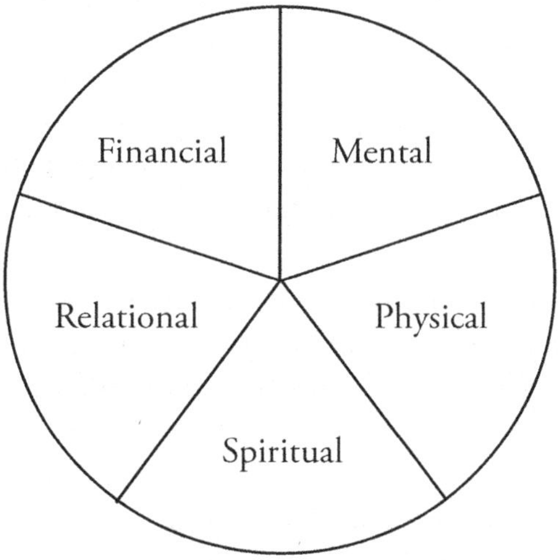

These are 5 areas of focus that enable me to make the greatest impact on my *Wheel of Life*:

- **Mental**: mental and emotional health; staying up-to-date and knowledgeable, learning, and growing (clinically and non-clinically)
- **Physical**: keeping my physical body healthy; managing my physical environment
- **Financial**: until your money is handled, you are not at choice in life
- **Spiritual**: the feeling, sense, or belief there is something greater than me, something more to being human than sensory experience, and the greater whole is cosmic or divine in nature

- **Relational**: state of being connected with others—family, friends, acquaintances, romantic, professional, group/community; maintaining 5 relationship boundaries (physical, emotional, sexual, intellectual, financial); compassionate love.

I invite you to step away from the *busyness and turmoil* of daily life and spend some personal time to reflect on what is working well and what needs your attention in terms of these five areas of your life—mental, physical, financial, spiritual, and relational. After you have examined each area and determined your short list of priorities to address and improve, choose one area upon which to focus for 21 to 30 days. Then identify one specific action you will begin taking consistently to improve in this focus area.

Our Human Needs Checklist

Use these descriptions of each human need to explore which of these are being met for you currently, and which ones are not. What can you stop doing, start doing, or continue doing to tap into your human needs?

- ☐ **Certainty**: This is the need for assurance that allows us to avoid pain and gain pleasure. It is the desire for stability and predictability in our lives. Examples include having a steady job, having a secure home, or having a routine that provides a sense of security.

- ☐ **Uncertainty/Variety**: This need is all about the desire for the unknown, change, and new stimuli. It is the need for excitement, adventure, and spontaneity. Examples include trying new activities, exploring new places, or engaging in hobbies that provide variety and diversity.

- ☐ **Significance**: This human need refers to the feeling of being unique, important, special, or needed. It is the need to be recognized and valued. Examples include being acknowledged for achievements, having a sense of purpose, or receiving praise and appreciation from others.

- ☐ **Connection/Love**: This is the need for a strong feeling of closeness or union with someone or something. It is the desire for meaningful relationships, love, and belonging. Examples include having close friendships, being part of a supportive community, or experiencing intimacy in a romantic relationship.

- ☐ **Growth**: This need involves the expansion of capacity, capability, or understanding. It is the desire for self-improvement, learning, and personal development. Examples include pursuing educational opportunities, setting personal goals, or engaging in activities that promote personal growth.

- ☐ **Contribution**: This human need is centered around a sense of service, focusing on helping, giving to, and supporting others. It is the desire to make a positive impact and leave a lasting legacy. Examples include volunteering, making charitable donations, or mentoring others in need.

CHAPTER 4

Bouncing Back from Burnout: Rebuilding Resilience

Burnout Symptoms and Stressors Checklist

US Surgeon General Vivek Murthy declared a "workplace loneliness epidemic" in 2017. This was before Covid! The World Health Organization declared burnout an official occupational phenomenon in 2019.

Burnout Symptoms

The following are the sixteen most common symptoms of burnout for dentists, according to various studies globally. Take note of which ones resonate for you.

- ☐ Emotional exhaustion
- ☐ Nagging, lingering frustrations
- ☐ Feeling completely spent at the end of the day
- ☐ Waking up late or not looking forward to another day at the office
- ☐ Chronic fatigue
- ☐ Sporadic mealtime, even skipping meals
- ☐ Cynicism
- ☐ Less sense of accomplishment
- ☐ Irritability
- ☐ Physical symptoms
- ☐ Isolation
- ☐ Substance overuse
- ☐ Less energized, motivated, or inspired by your work—loss of interest
- ☐ Feeling withdrawn, desensitized, or detached from your work and people
- ☐ Questioning yourself, lack of feeling competent
- ☐ Anxiety or racing thoughts

Burnout Stressors

- ☐ **Constant time pressure**: under constant time pressure as they attempt to provide quality treatment for their patients within the allotted time frame
- ☐ **No breaks**: little or no breaks from the high-pressure work environment.

- ☐ **Long hours**: enduring long hours requiring high levels of concentration. This can be taxing on their mental and physical health, with feelings of exhaustion, leading to fatigue and an overall decrease in job performance.
- ☐ **Monotony**: Doing the same thing over and over each day can lead to a sense of monotony that can contribute to burnout.
- ☐ **Financial pressures**: loans, mortgages, cash flow, receivables, and insurances can be intimidating for dentists.
- ☐ **Unresolved conflicts**: such as difficulties working with associates, team members, vendors/ suppliers and patients can be a major source of stress.
- ☐ **Self-criticism**: and recurring thoughts of mistakes, doubts and expectations can lead to feelings of inadequacy or insecurity. Dentists may have recurring thoughts or doubts about their ability to provide the highest standards of patient care, or whether they are up to date on the latest advancements in dentistry.
- ☐ **Unrealistic expectations**: self-imposed or imposed by others, for their own performance as business owner, leader, and dentist, can create high levels of stress as well.

Some of the biggest stressors linked to burnout are institutional or systems-based issues, yet many of them are personal belief and mindset challenges, and leadership opportunities.

Which stressors are negatively impacting you the most right now?

____

____

____

____

Which stressors do you have control over or the ability to change?

____

____

____

____

Which one of the leadership opportunities do you get to address (unresolved conflicts, lack of delegation, managing financial pressures)?

____

____

____

____

What specifically happens if you don't address any of these stressors for 30 more days?

____

____

____

____

Starting Your Own Private Mastermind Checklist

Three Keys to Mastermind Success

1. **Structure**: Keeping a structure to the meetings keeps them from devolving into nothing but social gatherings. Stand for structure for the sake of efficiency, effectiveness, and impact.

2. **People**: Choose carefully. Be sure to select people who are like-minded in terms of abundance mindset, generosity, commitment to personal growth and learning, and your own values.

3. **Commitment**: The group and its success must be a priority to you or don't waste your time starting one. If you truly understand the value of bringing like-minded professionals together who can support one another, then you will invest the time, enjoy the process, and benefit immensely.

- ☐ **Grounding**: Host and facilitate from a place of contribution, service, support, and abundance. Hold the space for your members as an exclusive safe confidential space to explore personal and professional challenges and opportunities.

- ☐ **Invitation**: Be selective and deliberate, you want 6-10 people in attendance. Always remember this is your event, your group. These people are potential clients, joint-venture partners, or sphere's of influence for you.

- ☐ **Video**: Video invitations on a private web page are the best way to deliver your invitations, next to making them in person with each prospective member.

- ☐ **Timing**: Typically you will host your group in the early morning or perhaps around the lunch hour. Hosting your group for 3-4 hours once every couple months, or quarterly, is best.

- ☐ **Purpose**: Be clear about the purpose and the goal of the group. Ensure you have everyone's buy-in for the group, and they see the value of the group the same as you.

- ☐ **Opening Questions**: At your first meeting, invite each member to contribute using four simple questions.
  - Brief background about you personally and professionally
  - Who do you help and how do you help them?
  - What projects are you working on now that excite you?
  - What support would be most helpful for you right now?

- ☐ **Private Group**: Whether you create a private FB group, use Slack, or skool, providing an online community can provide extra value. However, ask your members if they want this and whether they will use it, before you go to all the trouble to create one.

Types of Meetings to Host Within Your Mastermind Group

"Hot Seats" or "Spotlights"

Either in the large group, or in smaller groups, one member shares a challenge or opportunity they are facing. They provide only a couple minutes of background and specific details. The member then asks one specific, clear question on which they would like the other members to respond. Another member can serve as a notetaker so the member in the spotlight can simply focus on what is being said. The member does not need to say a word or, respond in any way to the various members providing feedback, except to say, "Thank you for the feedback." The member does not need to explain further or justify anything after receiving feedback. The only time a member will explain further is if another member(s) has a clarifying question for the spotlight member. Typically a member hot seat is 15-20 minutes in duration but can be shorter or longer.

Expert Content Presentations

This can be you, the host, sharing your expertise with the group, or another member presenting, or an invited subject matter expert. The power of these meetings is in the post-presentation facilitation and discussion amongst the members.

Develop a Team Goal

This can foster incredible collaboration and build deeper relationships amongst the members. The group commits to taking on a single project during the duration of the Mastermind Group. For example, the team may adopt a charity for 6-months and decide to conduct a fundraiser for the charity; or, pick a common challenge all members are facing and they decide to tackle it together over 30-90 days.

Various Leaders

For each meeting you can invite a member to present and/or facilitate a process, method, or exercise, that the group would benefit from working through together. Or the member may simply facilitate a meaningful discussion amongst the group. Sharing the leadership amongst the members brings the group together even closer, and members experience and learn from their fellow members in ways they may not have otherwise.

Speed Teaching or TEDx Format

For an hour of a meeting, for example, a select number of members each get 8 minutes to present a specific piece of expertise, and 2 minutes of Q&A with the group. It works best to have only 4 or 5 members present in a single hour. Information overload is a risk worthy of avoiding. In between each presentation, the host can facilitate a reflection exercise for each member, by inviting them to write down 1) biggest AHA or takeaway; 2) one thing they will change immediately because of the presentation; 3) what they will stop, start, or continue doing in light of the information shared in the presentation; and 4) identify one person or resource they need to pursue in order to take action on their takeaways.

Round Robin Discussions

This is time set aside for the entire group to meet, and for each member to share one item that is on their mind, either personal or professional in nature. The member can simply share something, give an update, or ask a question, seek specific feedback, or ask for resources or support in other ways. These are typically much shorter than hot seats. For example, each member may only have 4 minutes to share their thoughts and make their request or ask their question. Then the group has 5 minutes to reply, provide feedback, and discuss the member's issue.

On Location Visits

Monthly or quarterly meetings can be hosted at various members' business locations. Or the group can go on-site to visit a business for a tour and a post-tour discussion.

Report Out

One best practice to include in the opening of all Mastermind Group meetings is to first offer all members the opportunity to quickly (1-2 minutes) share the wins they have experienced since the last meeting.

CHAPTER 5

Success and Your Quality of Life
The Success Windows Reflection Exercise Worksheet

Determine What Matters Most

One way to get grounded in a post-win or post-fail reflective period is to commit a little time to revisiting where you're at now; what you desire; and, most importantly, why.

This *Success Windows Reflection Exercise* can be done on a piece of paper or on a whiteboard to help you quickly gain clarity about what truly matters to you personally.

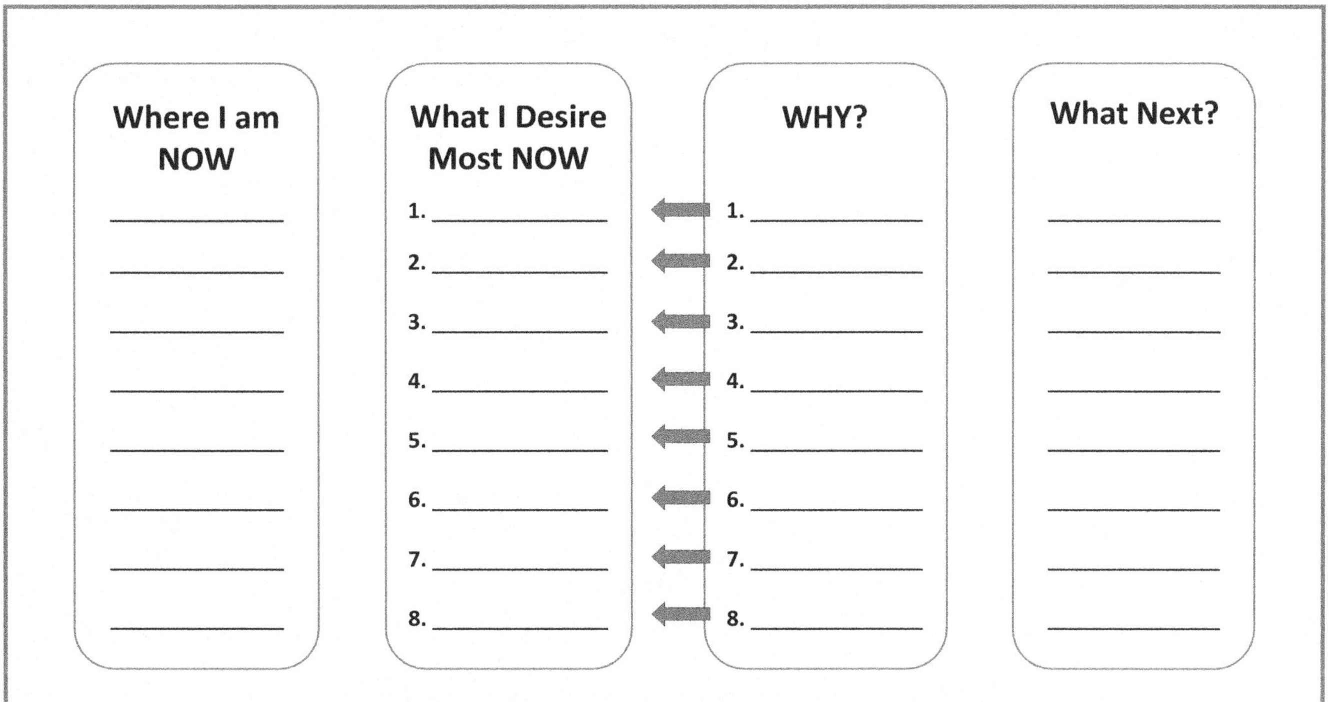

SUCCESS WINDOWS REFLECTION EXERCISE

In the first column, "Where I am NOW, "jot down everything that comes to mind about where you are now. This can be in your career, relationships, and/or anything that comes to mind. Just as fast as you can think of it, put it down on paper. This is called "fast writing."

Next, think about what you most want or desire currently. In the second column, "What I Desire Most Now," "fast write" everything you dream you could have right now.

Then in the third column, "WHY," jot down your answers to the question, "Why?", to each of the items on the second column, "What I Desire Most Now." As you do this, try to drill down deeper into each answer as to why this answer is important to you personally.

Example: "I want to buy a new car."

1. Why? "Because I earned it."
2. Why? "Because it will give me a sense of luxury for all my hard work."
3. Why? "Because I want to feel relaxed."
4. Why? "Because when I feel relaxed, I tap into total peace of mind."

You may find after drilling down deep enough that you don't need a new car because it will cost you more, leading to more time at work and, ultimately, giving you *less* peace of mind. You may find what you really want is more leisure time which is better realized without the added debt or cost of a new car.

However, maybe you get clear that the luxury car *is* important because you spend enough time in it that it's worth the expense. Whatever the outcome, the idea is to get completely clear about *WHY* anything you desire truly matters so you don't inadvertently chase a desire that takes you further away from the important things that matter most to you.

Often by revisiting in deep reflection your WHY beneath what you want, you can find yourself eliminating things you may have initially thought were important or replacing some items with more meaningful priorities.

Building a strategy to reach your goals is the easy part. Once you're clear on where you're at, what you want, and WHY, you are more likely to take action in pursuit of what you desire.

Where I am NOW	What I Desire Most NOW		WHY?	What Next?
______	1. ______	⟵	1. ______	______
______	2. ______	⟵	2. ______	______
______	3. ______	⟵	3. ______	______
______	4. ______	⟵	4. ______	______
______	5. ______	⟵	5. ______	______
______	6. ______	⟵	6. ______	______
______	7. ______	⟵	7. ______	______
______	8. ______	⟵	8. ______	______

SUCCESS WINDOWS REFLECTION EXERCISE

CHAPTER 6

The Power of Influence: Making a Positive Impact in Your World

Stop, Start, Continue Checklist

Two of the more powerful and effective tools to use in facilitating team meetings and individual meetings as well are, Stop, Start, Continue and Mad, Glad and Sad.

Some of the most common situations to use these tools in are:

- Teambuilding with staff or management teams
- Soliciting feedback from front-line staff
- Facilitating constructive coaching conversations with an individual
- Discussions with almost anyone when your need is to discover the "real issues" of a situation or a relationship

Stop, Start, Continue and Mad, Glad and Sad can be completed in private by groups of individuals, in dialogue with an individual, or as an interactive team exercise for an entire team simultaneously (using flipcharts for data capture).

1. Pass one copy of the Stop, Start, Continue form to each participant. Then ask everyone to quietly, with no discussion, read through the handout and then ask them to write down their responses to the following questions privately using the Stop, Start, Continue handout. You could then facilitate a group discussion, asking individual participants to share whatever they are comfortable sharing in discussion with the entire group.

2. This can be used with individuals in private one-on-one conversations as well in an effort to offer a tool to guide your discussion. You could send the form to the person in advance of your meeting as well if this makes your face-to-face time more meaningful and efficient.

3. Another method is to bring a group of 10-12 employees or managers together (traditionally this is not used with managers and staff in the same group—at least in the beginning of your use of this process). Using flipcharts around the room, one labeled STOP, one labeled START and one labeled CONTINUE, you simply ask everyone to either approach the flip chart pages and write their ideas down under each category, or use post it notes first—with one idea written per post-it, and then ask the participants to place their post-its on the flipchart pages under each category.

4. Examples of questions to use in the use of Stop, Start, Continue are:

    - What could we Stop, Start or Continue to do together as a department, to make this a better place to work?
    - What could I Stop, Start or Continue to do as your boss, to become an even better boss?
    - What do each of us need to Stop, Start or Continue doing in order to become more effective team members?
    - Thinking of the way in which this team communicates on a regular basis, what do we need to Stop, Start or Continue doing?

5. Examples of questions to use in the use of Mad, Glad and Sad are:

    - Thinking of your daily work life here at work, what are you Mad about, Glad about, and Sad about?
    - When you think of how our team interacts and supports each other, what are you Mad about, Glad about and Sad about?
    - When you think of how we treat our customers or patients, what are you Mad about, Glad about and Sad about?

6. The only "rules" to use when soliciting feedback from participants using these two tools:

    - If you provide an idea under one category, please offer another idea under one of the other categories—e.g., if you list a Stop, list a Start too; if you list a Mad, list a Glad too.
    - Your contribution must be genuine, constructive and sensitively worded.

Successful Collaboration Checklist

Navigating Successful Collaborations

Define Success

Be clear about the definition of success. Examples of important components to include in the definition of success are any combination of the following:

- ☐ Financial Expectations
- ☐ Timelines
- ☐ All Who Benefit
- ☐ The "Why" Behind the Collaboration
- ☐ Goal(s)
- ☐ Metrics to Measure
- ☐ Specific Language

Set Clear Expectations

Write out a detailed list of the expectations for each party. Expectations may include any combination of the following, or additional unique items.

Financial:

- ☐ Identify the cash, products, and resources each party is investing
- ☐ Decide who has the authority to make binding agreements and spend money

Ground Rules:

- ☐ Clearly define roles and responsibilities for each party
- ☐ Decide how decisions will be made when two parties are at an impasse
- ☐ Establish ground rules and/or behavioral standards

Timeframes:

- ☐ Specify deadlines and details for deliverables
- ☐ Detail projected dates of periodic milestones for the project

Additional Tips for Success

- ☐ Create a culture of trust and empowerment
- ☐ Recognize accomplishments
- ☐ Radical candor
- ☐ Radical responsibility
- ☐ Focus on win-win-win
- ☐ Create ground rules or behavior standards

- ☐ Clarify authority limits/boundaries—Promote autonomy
- ☐ Overcommunicate

Skills for Successful Collaborations

- ☐ Adaptability
- ☐ Empathy/Compassion
- ☐ Humility
- ☐ Willingness to Change
- ☐ Open to New Ideas
- ☐ Active Listening
- ☐ Radical Responsibility
- ☐ Radical Candor
- ☐ Timely Response and Follow Through
- ☐ Admit Mistakes, Learn and Move On

Team Engagement Best Practices Checklist

Here are some simple ways to stay engaged with your patients. Make note of which ones you aren't doing and could add to your repertoire for patients.

- ☐ Social media
- ☐ Newsletters
- ☐ Mail: celebrations, good-to-know tips
- ☐ Emails
- ☐ Reward/Loyalty programs
- ☐ Automated text and email reminders/recall
- ☐ Thank you notes/cards
- ☐ Blog articles
- ☐ Contests
- ☐ Referral rewards

Here are some simple ways to engage with your team:

- ☐ Team huddles
- ☐ Quarterly offsite team meetings
- ☐ One-on-one coaching for team leads
- ☐ Incentive programs
- ☐ Consistent acknowledgment
- ☐ Thank you notes/cards
- ☐ Employee appreciation experiences
- ☐ Additional training experiences
- ☐ Ask for their input and provide timely feedback
- ☐ Conduct Great Leader Conversation Starters™

Skills to ensure effective engagement:

- ☐ Supply the Right Tools
- ☐ Give Individual Attention
- ☐ Provide Training and Coaching
- ☐ Listen to Employees
- ☐ Get Social (business appropriate–no alcohol)
- ☐ Serve Others (servant leadership in support of them)
- ☐ Recognize Proudly and Loudly (celebrate publicly, coach privately)

Patient Engagement Best Practices Checklist

Perhaps use this checklist as an audit of what is working well for you right now, what needs to be improved, or what needs to be added to your patient engagement tactics.

- ☐ Patient Education: 46.67% of patient respondents reporting that patient education was the single most important factor in keeping patients engaged and returning to their practices.
- ☐ Enhance the Waiting Room Experience: 25% of patients switch providers because of poor digital experiences.
- ☐ Shared Decision-making for Personalized Patient Care Plans
- ☐ Quality Aftercare
- ☐ Early Engagement (before first appointment)
- ☐ Incentives and Rewards
- ☐ Engaging Website
- ☐ Online Scheduling
- ☐ Meaningful Social Media
- ☐ Send Out Reminders
- ☐ Implement Patient Surveys
- ☐ Follow Up (after appointments)
- ☐ Give Patients Access to Their Records and X-Rays
- ☐ Electronic Payments and Billing Options
- ☐ Encourage Open Communication
- ☐ Utilize Patient Reviews

Your People

CHAPTER 7

Retaining Valuable Team Members

Loyalty Self-Assessment Checklist

Before reviewing this list, think of one person on your team with whom you are unsure of their loyalty... to you, to their coworkers, to the business, or to your patients. This list may help you identify the potential source of your concern around their loyalty.

- ☐ **Strong Sense of Self**–secure with who they are, don't seek validation
- ☐ **No Triangulation nor Gossip**–keep confidences, don't complain behind their back
- ☐ **Assume the Best**–assume all parties have one another's best interest at heart
- ☐ **Intentions are Pure**–they communicate openly with no hidden agendas
- ☐ **They Fight Fair**–they care enough about you to resolve, not win, or defeat you
- ☐ **They Are Their Word**–they follow through and don't break promises
- ☐ **Collaborate**–they respect you and your talents and want to work together
- ☐ **Stand by You and For You**–they genuinely, sincerely support in good & bad times
- ☐ Seek First to Understand–then to be understood
- ☐ **Won't Always Agree**–yet will honestly share what they believe is best for you
- ☐ **Selfless**–they are givers who help others with no expectations
- ☐ **Boundaries**–they create a sense of mutual respect and protection
- ☐ **Values Commitment**–it's about dedication, determination, and conviction
- ☐ **Reliable**–they are dependable and strive to not disappoint those they value
- ☐ **Empathic**–they are sensitive to the needs of others
- ☐ **Keeps You in the Loop**–they communicate proactively and keep you informed

Six Staff Retention Drivers

Competitive Salaries
In order to retain employees in the dental profession, competitive salaries are essential. In 2023, dentists will need to make sure their salaries are in line with the industry standards and that they are offering incentives for employees who stay longer or take on additional responsibilities. Additionally, employers should consider offering bonuses and other forms of compensation in order to attract and retain top talent.

Flexible Scheduling
Flexible scheduling is also a key factor when it comes to keeping employees in the dental profession. Employees should be given the opportunity to work hours that fit their lifestyle and schedule, as this can help reduce stress levels and increase job satisfaction. Employers should also consider offering telecommuting options in order to give employees more freedom and flexibility when it comes to their work life balance.

Professional Development Opportunities
Providing professional development opportunities is another important way to retain employees in the dental profession. By offering courses, seminars, conferences, or other forms of training, employers can show their commitment to helping employees grow within the field and stay up-to-date on new developments.

Workplace Culture
The workplace culture is another important factor when it comes to staff retention in dentistry in 2023. Employers should strive to create an environment where employees feel valued, respected, and appreciated for their contributions. A positive workplace culture can help foster loyalty among employees and encourage them to stay with the organization for longer periods of time.

Job Security
Job security is a major factor when it comes to retaining staff in dentistry in 2023. Employees need assurance that they will have a stable job with long-term prospects so that they can plan ahead financially without worrying about losing their job unexpectedly due to economic downturns or other factors outside of their control. Employers should strive to provide job security by offering contracts or other forms of employment protection that guarantee job stability over time.

Benefits Packages
Finally, benefits packages play an important role when it comes to retaining staff in dentistry in 2023. Offering attractive benefits packages such as health insurance plans, retirement savings plans, paid vacation days, and other perks can help make an employer more appealing than competitors who do not offer such packages or offer less generous ones. This can be a great way for employers to differentiate themselves from others while also giving employees added incentive to remain with the organization over time.

Retaining Valuable Team Members Inventory

The following inventory items are meant for you to reflect upon them, asking yourself how well do you and or your team currently do this, or if absent, how can you add this to your processes and procedures or best practices. The focus of this inventory is a 360-degree look at the various factors and drivers of employee engagement and retention. As you read each declarative statement you can decide to what degree that is true for you, your team, your patients, or your practice.

1. All team members know and understand the vision and mission of my practice.
2. All team members know and understand the definition of success for our practice as a business, and in terms of the services we provide for our patients.
3. All team members know and understand the values of the organization and how they are expected to perform based on these values.
4. All team members know what is expected of them at work in terms of how they are to contribute to the success of the business.
5. We consistently provide the tools our employees need to fulfill their job duties at a level of excellence.
6. Our recruitment process consistently finds high-quality candidates who are well-suited to our business's culture and values.
7. Our recruitment process is excellent, including job postings, interviews, background checks, reference checks, post-interview follow-up, job offer conversations, and the speed at which we fill our open positions.
8. Our onboarding process is provided consistently and timely for all newly hired team members.
9. Our onboarding process reinforces to the new hire they made the right choice by joining the team.
10. Our onboarding process provides new hires with adequate training & resources necessary for success in their roles. This helps ensure they understand expectations from day one, reducing stress levels & increasing productivity among team members.
11. We consistently offer ongoing training opportunities for all team members to stay up to date on new technologies, procedures, and regulations in the dental industry.
12. Our regular training sessions allow employees to develop new skills that can help them advance within our practice or make them more marketable if they decide to pursue other employment outside our organization.
13. Tuition reimbursement programs or other forms of financial assistance is available for team members to pursue higher education or certifications that will benefit both themselves and the practice as a whole.
14. We have created a positive work environment.
15. We have created a culture where everyone feels valued and respected regardless of their role within the team.
16. We provide ample opportunities for collaboration between departments or teams within the practice itself.
17. We have created a collaborative environment where everyone is encouraged to contribute ideas, share knowledge, and offer solutions to problems they encounter during their day-to-day tasks at work.

18. There is healthy open communication between management and staff where everyone feels comfortable expressing their ideas or concerns without fear of retribution or judgment from their peers or supervisors.
19. We have created a culture that supports and enables team members to easily have peer-to-peer conversations regarding job duties or working conditions at the practice.
20. Our dentists recognize employee achievements in genuine ways, appropriate to the team member, and in a timely manner. This could be verbal recognition, thank you notes, awards, bonuses, promotions, mentorship opportunities or other rewarding experiences.
21. We offer flexible scheduling options such as flexible hours, telecommuting options when possible and appropriate, or compressed work weeks.
22. We offer competitive compensation, ensuring salaries and benefits packages are competitive with those offered by other organizations in the industry and in our local marketplace.
23. We offer competitive health insurance plans, retirement plans, vacation days, sick leave policies, and other employee benefits that contribute to our team members' feeling valued and appreciated.
24. Performance evaluations are conducted once or twice a year and are meaningful productive conversations providing feedback on areas of improvement, celebrating what is working well, and where additional training may be necessary.
25. We provide career advancement opportunities such as job shadowing programs, mentorship initiatives, leadership training courses, or other professional development opportunities.
26. We conduct an employee engagement survey at least once a year to gain insight into how employees feel about their job and the organization as a whole, e.g., job satisfaction, work environment, career development opportunities, and other employee retention topics.
27. We provide feedback in a timely manner to all team members after compiling the results of the employee engagement survey, including offering the initiatives we are undertaking immediately, within 30 days or more, in response to the data.
28. We provide recognition and rewards programs that recognize employees for outstanding performance or going above and beyond in their job duties. Our rewards are more experience based (coffee with the owner, tickets to a local theme park) rather than based on giveaways such as logo merchandise and physical gifts. Experiences are far more valuable in recognition and employee engagement and retention efforts.
29. We provide a mentorship program which pairs experienced staff members with new hires, allowing them to learn from each other & develop skills necessary for success within the practice.
30. We offer job security by providing clear pathways for advancement within the practice, ensuring that staff members have the opportunity to grow professionally within the organization rather than seeking employment elsewhere.
31. We organize regular team building activities outside of work such as group outings, picnics, sports tournaments, etc., which allow staff members to socialize outside of work & build strong relationships with one another .
32. We have established workplace safety protocols which protect both physical health of staff members (e.g., ergonomic furniture) as well as mental health (e.g., stress management techniques), creating a safe working environment where everyone feels comfortable expressing themselves without fear of repercussions from management.
33. We provide growth opportunities through promotions & additional responsibilities so that staff members can develop professionally within the organization rather than looking outside it for advancement opportunities.

34. We have established a paid time off policy which allows staff members to take time off when needed without worrying about financial repercussions and reducing stress levels associated with taking unpaid leave due to personal matters (e.g., tending to a sick family member).
35. We consistently offer opportunities for team members and their supervisors to meet one-on-one to build rapport, deepen their understanding of one another, and communicate openly.

Team Engagement Best Practices Checklist

Here are some simple ways to stay engaged with your patients. Make note of which ones you aren't doing and could add to your repertoire for patients.

- ☐ Social media
- ☐ Newsletters
- ☐ Mail: celebrations, good-to-know tips
- ☐ Emails
- ☐ Reward/Loyalty programs
- ☐ Automated text and email reminders/recall
- ☐ Thank you notes/cards
- ☐ Blog articles
- ☐ Contests
- ☐ Referral rewards

Here are some simple ways to engage with your team:

- ☐ Team huddles
- ☐ Quarterly offsite team meetings
- ☐ One-on-one coaching for team leads
- ☐ Incentive programs
- ☐ Consistent acknowledgment
- ☐ Thank you notes/cards
- ☐ Employee appreciation experiences
- ☐ Additional training experiences
- ☐ Ask for their input and provide timely feedback
- ☐ Conduct Great Leader Conversation Starters™

Skills to ensure effective engagement:

- ☐ Supply the Right Tools
- ☐ Give Individual Attention
- ☐ Provide Training and Coaching
- ☐ Listen to Employees
- ☐ Get Social (business appropriate–no alcohol)
- ☐ Serve Others (servant leadership in support of them)
- ☐ Recognize Proudly and Loudly (celebrate publicly, coach privately)

How to Accelerate Your Hiring
&
The Best Interview Questions Checklist

Accelerating Your Hiring Process

1. Write better job postings with more details and list salary range.
2. Schedule times and dates for each step of the process before ending the initial conversation.
3. When leaving a voicemail for a candidate, be aspirational and energetic.
4. Provide online questions with the ability for video responses from the candidate. There are plenty of online platforms available to do this.
5. When using FB Jobs, boost your posts.
6. Create a Youtube video, or a video on your website which accurately describes what it's like to work there, what a new hire can expect, and what the benefits are of joining your organization. Including staff members in this video adds credibility to the message.
7. Utilize telephone and zoom interviews to streamline the process compared to requiring all interviews to occur in person.
8. Conduct group interviews of 3 candidates pursuing the same position.
9. Be sure to leverage Glassdoor, Healthgrades, and Indeed platforms.
10. Candidate engagement: most will leave the process within 7 to 10 days if they are not happy with the experience. How the relationship starts is usually how it ends.
11. Re-recruit former great team members 90 days after they left your organization. Oftentimes they will realize the "grass is not always greener" at the new job and will be willing to return.
12. Get creative: Use community fairs, church/mosque/synagogue events, or even visit hospital employee parking lots to find high-quality candidates.

The Best Interview Questions Checklist

The following interview questions have been proven by multiple companies and research studies to provide great results in your interviewing efforts. You may also wish to research the world-class approach to interviewing known as Behavioral Based Interviewing. It is a completely different approach to asking interview questions which allows the candidate to speak more about the experience and practical knowledge than most interview formats.

1. What did you do to prepare for this interview? (Former CEO of Yahoo discovered this to be one of the most powerful productive opening questions in an interview.)
2. Tell me about yourself.
3. What's the coolest thing you've seen in the last 6 months?
4. What do you own that you love?
5. What gives you the most fulfillment in what you do?
6. What are the 2 or 3 superpowers you rely on the most?
7. What do you expect from us as an employer?
8. Why do you want to work with us?
9. Why did you leave your last job?
10. Tell me about your strengths and weaknesses.
11. What are your salary requirements?
12. What questions do you have about this job?

Three examples of behavioral-based interview questions:

- Share an experience which you used new training skills, ideas, or a method to adapt to a new situation or improve an ongoing one. (look for their ability to learn)

- Provide a time when you worked in a rapidly evolving workplace. How did you deal with the change? Be as specific as possible. (look for flexibility)

- Describe an experience in which you successfully controlled the operation of a difficult system. What specifically made you successful? (look for specifics)

Dental Associate Interview Template

GENERAL INFORMATION

Name ____ DDS DMD

Address: ____

Phone: ______________________ Phone: ______________________

Email: ______________________ Pager: ______________________

CREDENTIALS

____

______________________ (UNIVERSITY) ____________ (YEAR) ________

______________________ (UNIVERSITY) ____________ (YEAR) ________

______________________ (UNIVERSITY) ____________ (YEAR) ________

STUDY CLUBS

Name: ____

Name: ____

MEMBERSHIPS

Check boxes (list ones you want to know)

Other: ____

CONTINUING EDUCATION

____

____

____

CURRENT STATUS

□ UNEMPLOYED □ NEW GRAD □ RESIDENCY □ ASSOCIATE □ PARTNER

How long? ____

INTERVIEW QUESTIONS

What did you do to prepare for this interview?

What prompted you to contact me for this opportunity?

Why are you pursuing this Associate opportunity now?

Is there a reason you are looking for an opportunity in this area?

As a manager of the practice, what do you see your role to be?

What education do you believe you will need in the first year of your Associate role?

Clinical:

Management:

What is your long-term vision for yourself, say 5-10 years from now?

What are your biggest frustrations working as an Associate?

What 2 or 3 superpowers will you rely on to be an effective Associate?

What is the coolest thing you've seen in the past 6 months?

What do you expect from us as an employer?

What do you expect from me as the owner of this practice?

Are you looking for full-time or part-time employment?

How many days per week do you want to work?

How would you fill in your downtime to be most productive and effective?

Have you been an Associate at other practices?

Who was the principal doctor?

How long were you an Associate?

What did you like about this experience?

What did you like least about this experience?

What would you have changed to improve your experience?

CHAPTER 8

Mastering the Art of Asking Better Questions

Discovery and Breakthrough Questions Guide

Therefore, I figured out a few best ways to help my team members learn, ultimately, so I could delegate more to them with the confidence from knowing they will handle things correctly.

- Take note of tasks or issues that keep coming up repeatedly
- Pick one to address with the team that week
- Host a 5- or 10-minute huddle with the relevant team members, asking them for suggestions, recommendations
- Ask questions of them…avoid the temptation to tell them the solution even when you are "crazy busy"
- Invite them to come up with the solution for this issue that keeps coming up, and present their recommendations to you
- Then "trial" their solution
- Upon success with the "trial," document the process and add it to your communication and/or training procedures

Example: Team members frequently complain they can't find supplies in the inventory closet.

Instead of doing what seems to be "the easy thing to do," and just tell them exactly what to do to fix the problem, ask them to come up with the root cause of the issue, and recommend a solution.

Useful Discovery Questions to Ask Your Team Members:

- What are all the possible reasons XYZ is currently happening?
- Who are all the people/roles involved in making this happen?
- When does the problem happen most often?
- Where is the problem happening most often?
- What is the real problem? Are we addressing the "correct" problem?
- If you could change any one thing immediately about _____, what would you change?
- Are we asking the right question(s)?
- What happens if nothing changes, and we keep doing it the way we are doing it now?
- What is that costing us? (time, energy, delays, frustrations, poor Patient experience/outcomes)
- What is the ideal result we want to have happening instead?

- What should we stop doing, start doing or continue doing?
- What is the question we aren't asking that we should be asking?
- Who needs to be involved in addressing this?
- What knowledge, information, experience, tools, expert, resources do we need to improve this situation?
- What is the exact, step-by-step, best solution to resolve this problem once and for all? (short-term fix vs. long-term fix)
- What do the team members need from others to resolve this problem and keep it from happening again?
- Who are all the "others" that need to be made aware or be involved in the resolution of the problem, and the new process or procedures moving forward?
- How would you like to resolve this issue?

Whenever a team member says to you, in response to your question, "I don't know," simply respond, "Well if you did know, what would you do?"

Another great technique is to help the person see the issue from another perspective than their own. Ask them, "So if you were another person involved in this instead of you, what would that person say? Recommend?"

And finally, ask the individual or group of team members, "If you were the owner of this practice, what would you do?" Or asked a different way, "What would you do if you were me?"

Asking these questions provides a bunch of benefits, both short-term and long-term. Here are benefits we have experienced whenever we engage our team members (challenge and/or delegate) to find the solutions:

- Employees feel trusted and valued for their opinion and contribution
- Employees feel respected because you are asking for their input
- Employees feel empowered because they are now part of the solution
- These problems are resolved "once-and-for-all" reducing dysfunction, improving outcomes, increasing productivity, reducing stress et al
- Over time, employees stop coming to you with their questions and instead rely on one another to find the answers, or create solutions
- You witness/discover emerging leaders from within your team who step up as leaders during this entire process
- Time savings for everyone, especially you, are created, and last as long as the team continues to practice the new solution

Once you and your team have agreed upon and implemented the new procedure, new process, or whatever type of solution, you may want to check-in with your team member(s) using any of these following questions.

To ensure they understand and are committed to the solution:

- Do you understand what and why we are doing ______?
- Are you perfectly clear about _________?
- Are you comfortable with __________?
- Do you agree with our solution?

- Do you think this new approach will solve the problem? Short- and Long-term?
- Can you accomplish this as we have discussed it?
- Can you complete it on time?
- What aspects of this new procedure/solution are you most concerned about?
- Can you see anything that will get in the way, delay or derail our progress?

Another proactive approach to grow your people professionally and personally, which in turn often enables you to delegate more tasks and responsibilities to your team members, is to facilitate "breakthroughs" with your team members or the team as a whole.

Thomas Leonard, founder of CoachU, developed the following questions and follow-up questions to facilitate a breakthrough. All along the way of this journey to a breakthrough, are great chances for your team members to grow and develop their critical thinking skills.

7 Questions to Facilitate a Breakthrough:

1. What's the breakthrough you'd like to have with this (problem, issue, concern, opportunity)?
2. What needs to happen for this breakthrough to occur?
3. If you knew the answer, what would it be? (Follow up Question, Please tell me the first thing that comes to mind.)
4. What's in the way of you taking the next step or making a decision on this?
5. What do you gain by staying stuck or not taking action?
6. If you were advising a coworker about this situation, what would you say?
7. What's the next action you could take based on our discussion?

Follow Up Questions to Ask:

1. Tell me more about that (a prompt more than a question)
2. What did you just discover?
3. What are you present to now?
4. How would that make a difference?
5. What would achieving this breakthrough mean to you?

CHAPTER 9

Feedback Fuels Team Success

Stop, Start, Continue Checklist

Two of the more powerful and effective tools to use in facilitating team meetings and individual meetings as well are, Stop, Start, Continue and Mad, Glad and Sad.

Some of the most common situations to use these tools in are:

- Teambuilding with staff or management teams
- Soliciting feedback from front-line staff
- Facilitating constructive coaching conversations with an individual
- Discussions with almost anyone when your need is to discover the "real issues" of a situation or a relationship

Stop, Start, Continue and Mad, Glad and Sad can be completed in private by groups of individuals, in dialogue with an individual, or as an interactive team exercise for an entire team simultaneously (using flipcharts for data capture).

1. Pass one copy of the Stop, Start, Continue form to each participant. Then ask everyone to quietly, with no discussion, read through the handout and then ask them to write down their responses to the following questions privately using the Stop, Start, Continue handout. You could then facilitate a group discussion, asking individual participants to share whatever they are comfortable sharing in discussion with the entire group.

2. This can be used with individuals in private one-on-one conversations as well in an effort to offer a tool to guide your discussion. You could send the form to the person in advance of your meeting as well if this makes your face-to-face time more meaningful and efficient.

3. Another method is to bring a group of 10-12 employees or managers together (traditionally this is not used with managers and staff in the same group—at least in the beginning of your use of this process). Using flipcharts around the room, one labeled STOP, one labeled START and one labeled CONTINUE, you simply ask everyone to either approach the flip chart pages and write their ideas down under each category, or use post it notes first—with one idea written per post-it, and then ask the participants to place their post-its on the flipchart pages under each category.

4. Examples of questions to use in the use of Stop, Start, Continue are:

    - What could we Stop, Start or Continue to do together as a department, to make this a better place to work?
    - What could I Stop, Start or Continue to do as your boss, to become an even better boss?
    - What do each of us need to Stop, Start or Continue doing in order to become more effective team members?
    - Thinking of the way in which this team communicates on a regular basis, what do we need to Stop, Start or Continue doing?

5. Examples of questions to use in the use of Mad, Glad and Sad are:

    - Thinking of your daily work life here at work, what are you Mad about, Glad about, and Sad about?
    - When you think of how our team interacts and supports each other, what are you Mad about, Glad about and Sad about?
    - When you think of how we treat our customers or patients, what are you Mad about, Glad about and Sad about?

6. The only "rules" to use when soliciting feedback from participants using these two tools:

    - If you provide an idea under one category, please offer another idea under one of the other categories—e.g., if you list a Stop, list a Start too; if you list a Mad, list a Glad too.
    - Your contribution must be genuine, constructive and sensitively worded.

Co-Creating Behavior Standards Checklist

Tips for Designing and Implementing Behavior Standards:

- ☐ They are also referred to as Standards of Performance, Performance Standards or Standards in Practice.
- ☐ Become crystal clear about what your vision is for implementing these standards, what you are trying to accomplish, and why you are doing it.
- ☐ Seek input from all employees in creating the document. This takes time but is the most valuable aspect of the process for ensuring employee buy-in later which is priceless.
- ☐ Align desired behaviors with organizational goals and desired outcomes—make sure the priorities match and ring true.
- ☐ Review other organizations' Standards of Behavior—study the successful implementations of others.
- ☐ Be crystal clear and very specific in your wording. Say exactly what you mean and avoid colloquialisms and jargon. For instance, state, "make eye contact, smile and verbally greet all guests who come within five feet of you at any time."
- ☐ Hold a ceremonial Standards of Behavior "roll out." Have all existing employees sign their commitment to the new Standards.
- ☐ Hold people accountable when they violate a standard. Model the importance of these standards consistently and endlessly, by senior and middle management.
- ☐ Create a designated "Standard of the Month." Post and distribute liberally throughout the organization for the first 12 months after initial introduction.
- ☐ Update the Standards of Behavior over time to keep them current.
- ☐ Have new applicants sign it right up front—preview it on your website and job application, review it in the interview process and then have the new hire sign their commitment on their first day of orientation to the company.
- ☐ Keep your list of Standards to no more than 7 with brief, clear descriptions of the behavior expected for this standard.

Sample Behavioral Standards

Respect

- Patients First is our Focus
- Respect and honor our employees and physicians
- Model mutual respect by caregivers and leaders

Privacy and Confidentiality

- Maintain confidentiality of patient information at all times
- Respect the privacy needs of our patients
- Conduct appropriate conversations at all times

Quality

- Provide exceptional clinical care to every patient we serve
- Fully embrace the patient's Right To Know
- Demonstrate commitment to continuous improvement

Professionalism

- Serve as a role model of Company at all times
- Choose your attitude daily, with Patients and Guests in mind · Look and act the part of a health care professional always

Safety

- Provide a clean, healthy and safe environment
- Work smarter, think Safety first

Communication

- Fully explain care procedures to our patients in advance
- Be sensitive to the individual needs of our patients
- Keep patients informed about their care throughout their stay
- Listen to and share information in a timely manner between co-workers

Teamwork

- Provide exceptional responsiveness from our staff
- All share in the commitment to co-workers for effective teamwork
- Support the goals of the organization

Accountability

- Everyone takes pride in the work we do and the services we provide
- Each of us holds ourselves accountable in providing exceptional care to our patients
- Each team member is accountable for their own choices

CHAPTER 10

Great Leader Conversation Starters to Engage Your Team Members

Great Leader Conversation Starters®
Guide and Checklist
One-on-One Team Member Conversations that Make a Difference

BEST PRACTICES CHECKLIST

- ☐ Near the end of every one-on-one meeting, ask, "What can you do to take action or make progress on what we discussed today?" or, "What are 2 or 3 specific actions you can take to move forward on what we discussed today, and by when?"

- ☐ The leader's role in a one-on-one is to draw out the issues, concerns and opportunities from the team member, by asking questions and then actively listening.

- ☐ Don't rush them, schedule at least 30 minutes, and keep the appointment unless it is <u>imperative</u> to reschedule—rescheduling oftentimes erodes trust and negatively impacts engagement.

- ☐ Share a time you made a mistake or learned a lesson from failing, or simply model the type of response you are looking for from your team member by sharing your own experience, e.g., "I remember a lesson I learned from my first job which was XYZ, and that has helped me in _____ way ever since. What is a lesson you learned from one of your previous jobs?"

- ☐ Remember, Peter Drucker's sound advice, "Unless commitment is made, there are only promises and hopes, but no plans."

Great Leader Conversation Starters®

QUESTIONS

FOSTERING COMMUNICATION & FEEDBACK

1. Describe the work environment and culture in which you could most successfully do your best work? How far from ideal is your current workplace?
2. What is the single most significant factor interfering with our success (that our company can control)? What factor fuels our success as a company?
3. What's a lesson you learned earlier in your career from a mistake you made or a failure you experienced?
4. If you could change any one thing immediately about ____________ what would you change?
5. What form of communication works best for you? (Visual, Auditory, Tactile)
6. Do you prefer email, text, phone call, voicemail, in-person face-to-face?
7. Do you feel you are getting enough feedback? How often do you want to receive feedback from your manager? …your team members? (almost daily, weekly, monthly, quarterly, annually)
8. What could I do to make your work easier? What feedback do you have for me so I can be a more effective leader—what can I do better?

DISCOVERING WHAT DRIVES OTHER PEOPLE

1. What would you most like to be remembered for when you retire/no longer work here?
2. What is your best way to start your day and end your day?
3. What drives you? What motivates you to come to work each day?
4. What activity outside of work restores your energy, so you avoid burnout?
5. Are you able to make this a "must-have" in your daily life now?
6. Are you more energized working on projects with other people first, or do you prefer, first working alone, and then connecting with others?
7. At work, most of the time, are you more fast-paced or slower-paced in terms of walking, talking, decision making, completing tasks?
8. Are you more open (extroverted) or guarded (introverted), most of the time at work?
9. At the end of the day, when you look back on the day, do you measure your own success at work based upon:

   A) the work you got accomplished yourself;

   B) the work you got accomplished with and through others;

   C) the relationships and people you engaged/impacted;

   D) the systems and processes you engaged with and impacted?

10. Which is more important to you most of the time, the quality of work you complete, or the quantity of work you complete?

INCREASING TRUST WITH EACH OTHER

1. What was your first job and what was one lesson you learned from that job experience?
2. What is the most important thing you have learned in the last year?
3. What drains your energy at work? What energizes you at work?
4. What's one thing we could change about work for you that would improve your personal life?
5. What did you do for fun in the past that you haven't had as much time for lately?
6. What advice would you give to a 22-year-old version of yourself?

ENCOURAGING PARTICIPATION & ENGAGEMENT

1. Do you get to do something at work every day that you love? If so, what is it? If not, what can you do about that?
2. What's your go-to productivity trick?
3. What's one thing we could do differently here to make your work more efficient? ...rewarding? ... meaningful? ...productive?
4. Is your job what you expected when you accepted it?
5. When was the time you enjoyed working here the most?
6. Are you happy working here now? Are you happy with your most recent work?
7. Is there anything you contribute to this team that you believe is undervalued or underappreciated?
8. What part of your job do you wish you didn't have to do? What do you enjoy most about working here?

CAREER DEVELOPMENT

1. What work are you doing here you feel is most in line with your long-term goals?
2. What do you want to be doing here in 3 years? ...5 years? ...10 years? How can we help you achieve those goals?
3. If you had millions of dollars, what would you do every day?
4. What do you want to do in your next job/role?
5. Do you feel challenged at work? Are you learning new things?
6. What area of the company/other jobs would you like to learn more about?
7. What skills would you like to develop right now?
8. Who in the company would you like to learn from? What do you want to learn?
9. What additional training, education or orientation would you like?

Progress Check-in Questions

1. Do you feel like you are making progress toward your long-term goals at work?
2. Are we helping you advance your career at the pace you prefer? If not, how can we support you moving forward?
3. What would need to change to enable you to make more progress on your biggest goals at work?
4. What is something you want to do in the next year, that you have never done before?
5. How could we better leverage your unique skill set for the benefit of our customers, our company and our team members?

IMPROVEMENT: Our Company

1. What should the company be doing today to better compete in the market?
2. What's one thing we "got to do" in the next 6 months to improve our product/service?
3. If you were me, or the CEO, what's the first thing you would change?
4. What's the #1 challenge at our company right now? Why? What do you suggest we do to address this?
5. Based on your daily experience, what does our company truly value, not just espouse to value?

IMPROVEMENT: Our Team

1. How could we improve our team meetings?
2. Do you feel over-worked, under-worked or just right?
3. Do you feel you are on the same page with your team? If no, what needs to improve?
4. Are there any meetings or communications you think you should be included in that you are not currently included? Are there any meetings you don't want to be a part of now?
5. Is everyone pulling their weight on the team?
6. Who on the team do you have the most difficulty working with and why?
7. Are you uncomfortable giving any of your peer's constructive feedback?
8. If you could change one thing immediately about how your team works together, what would you change?

ONE-on-ONE QUESTIONS TO ASK A MANAGER/SUPERVISOR

MANAGER'S EXPERIENCE

1. Do you spend too much time in meetings? If yes, which meetings do you think you should stop attending? Is there someone on your team who could/should attend in your place?
2. Divided by percentages, how much of your day, on average, is spent in meetings; managing your team; completing your own work alone; putting out fires/doing work that could be done by others in your department/team; coaching team members? (e.g., 40% meetings; 10% managing team; 20% completing own work; 25% putting out fires/doing work of others; 5% coaching)
3. If money were no obstacle, what investment would help you be even more effective as a leader of your team?
4. Most of the time, do you receive enough support from your peers? If not, what needs to improve?
5. If you were me, what changes would you make?

ONE-on-ONE QUESTIONS TO ASK A MANAGER/SUPERVISOR

MANAGER ENGAGEMENT & SATISFACTION

1. Is your role and your daily work experience what you thought it would be a year ago?
2. Do you have the tools and resources you need to effectively lead your team?
3. Do I provide enough support and timely follow-up for you?
4. What do I need to stop doing or start doing to better support you?
5. What feedback do I need to hear that you think no one has had the courage to tell me until now?
6. How do you feel about the amount of time you are able to spend developing your team, coaching team members and focusing on building effective systems, processes, procedures for our future success?
7. Are you happy in this role right now? Why or why not? What needs to change?
8. Do you feel you are spending more time putting out fires, or building a self-directed team?
9. Do you take all your allotted vacation time each year? Why or why not?
10. Do you have a mentor/coach within the company, other than me?

ONE-on-ONE QUESTIONS TO ASK A MANAGER/SUPERVISOR

MANAGER AS COACH

1. What issue/skill/concern keeps coming up within your team which you think would be improved by providing more training? ...what specific training do you suggest?
2. Are you able to meet one-on-one with each team member often enough? Why or why not?
3. Who are your best performers? Are we providing enough opportunities for them to learn new things, grow their responsibility, or become ready for a promotion?
4. Who is struggling or is at risk due to their performance, right now? What action plan is in place?
5. What's the best suggestion or most innovative idea your team has shared with you recently?
6. Is anyone ready for promotion or additional responsibility right now? Specifically, what else do they need to ensure their success?
7. What is your biggest challenge/concern based on the coaching conversations you have had with your team members?
8. Have any of your team members completed job shadowing in other departments in the past 90 days? If no, why, and what needs to happen so job shadowing can occur more consistently?

ONE-on-ONE QUESTIONS TO ASK A MANAGER/SUPERVISOR

TEAM FOCUS

1. What are 3 of your team's biggest successes in the past 30 days? 90 days?
2. What is the definition of success for your team—operationally and financially? ...product/service-wise? ...within the team? ...with other teams/departments?
3. What are you most proud of about your team right now?
4. If you could change any one thing immediately about the performance of your team, what would you change?
5. What's the biggest obstacle/challenge keeping your team from producing better results? ...collaborating better amongst themselves?
6. If money were no obstacle, what investment would you request to be made to help your team?

Employee Engagement and Retention Checklist

As you reflect upon this list, identify what you and your people are already doing well, and what they can improve on in order to best engage your employees and boost employee retention.

The Core Factors of Successful Employee Engagement are:

- ☐ Trust, Rapport, and Feedback
- ☐ Belonging, Purpose, Meaning
- ☐ Happiness, Fulfillment, and Worth
- ☐ Progress and Learning
- ☐ Achievement, Energy, and Collaboration
- ☐ Career Development
- ☐ Continuous Improvement

Team Chat Sessions® Success Guide and Checklist
"Team Member Only" Small Group Discussions

BEST PRACTICES CHECKLIST

The Success Framework for TEAM CHATS:

- ○ Schedule up to 5 team members per session
- ○ Make sure session happens, even if someone can't make it
- ○ Set the ground rules
- ○ Invite them to share with you the 1-3 biggest takeaways from their discussion—suggestions, concerns, feedback, questions, aha's, mindset shifts, plans or requests

Ground Rules for Success (examples):

- ○ Stay on topic—no tangents, long stories, or "going down rabbit holes"
- ○ One person speaks at a time, listen actively
- ○ Share the air-time—no one person dominates conversation
- ○ Assume the best in each other and their intention in sharing
- ○ No cellphone usage of any kind, no audio/video recording of any kind
- ○ Do not discuss anything from your conversation, especially "who said what" outside of this session—gossip kills trust—exception: sharing feedback with your manager or senior leader
- ○ Conduct TEAM CHAT Session in a private space, away from other team members, e.g., private conference room
- ○ Speak for yourself from your experience only, do not try to speak for others; no blaming or labeling
- ○ Always be professional, constructive and mature
- ○ No gossip or triangulation (speaking of someone not present)
- ○ Start on time, end on time
- ○ If someone arrives late, they do the Hokey Pokey (all verses)
- ○ Provide the 1-3 takeaways (mentioned above) in writing, to your manager, before the end of business, on same day
- ○ Embrace possibility—focus conversation on what <u>can</u> be done rather than just stewing in what can't be done or "all the problems;" be solutions and progress focused

BEST PRACTICES CHECKLIST PART 2

- ☐ Keep track of who attends each session to get as many team members involved as possible over time—some may attend multiple sessions.
- ☐ Select topic for sessions based on current challenges, opportunities or initiatives.
- ☐ Keep the first sessions to 15-20 minutes, then extend over time if necessary.
- ☐ Thank all team members for attending and participating in these sessions.
- ☐ Have fun yet keep the discussion professional and work focused.
- ☐ Invite one of your top performers, or promotion candidates to facilitate the discussion—at first, co-facilitating the session with them, then releasing them to conduct these sessions on their own, following your team's guidelines, expectations and ground rules.
- ☐ Never audio or video record Team Chat Sessions® without signed Audio and Video Release forms, signed by every participant in advance of the session.
- ☐ One great method for receiving feedback from the team after their session is to ask them to provide their input regarding what we as a team or department need to Stop, Start or Continue doing (do not single out individuals' names in this feedback).

COMMUNICATION & FEEDBACK

1. If you want better results, ask better questions.
2. A leader's job is to take their team members on a journey of discovery, by asking more questions, not just telling them what to do.
3. How are we doing with passing on information between shifts—days, evenings and nights? … between weekend team members and weekday team members?
4. At work, when could I be more courageous?
5. What am I pretending not to notice about myself at work?
6. The greatest gift anyone can receive is constructive feedback on their behavior.
7. If you could change any one thing immediately about ____________, what would you change? (no limit on resources)

Identify a specific topic to put into the blank above. Then listen to your team members' responses. Remember, responding to them by asking "Can you tell me more about that?" is far better than asking "Why did you say that?"

8. What would you do if you were me?

Perhaps the "me" is the team's direct supervisor/manager. Or team members can pair off and ask this question of one another.

WHAT DRIVES PEOPLE

1. People's deepest desire is to be understood.
   - People want to be heard, understood and cared for
   - How do we each do that for one another?
2. What you focus on, you find.
3. What would you most like to be remembered for when you retire or no longer work here?
4. Stop letting others' petty, minor complaints become your major focus. Choose your response and you will change your life.

INCREASED TRUST

You may wish to provide a facilitator for these discussions regarding trust.

1. Every choice creates an outcome.

   "I never fail, I create outcomes." –Dennis McIntee

   What's one choice you need to make today to create a different outcome? Do you need any support from others?

2. This is a safe place where I can fail and learn from my failures, without fearing that I will lose my job.
   - Is this true for you, based on your experience here so far? If yes, what specifically makes you feel it is safe to fail and learn from your failures here?
   - If no, what needs to happen so you may feel safe at some point in the future?

3. What am I grateful for?

INCREASED TRUST

4. When I have a challenge at work, I feel supported and have access to the resources I need to address the challenge myself.
   - If you agree, what makes this so for you?
   - If you disagree, what support and/or resources would help you the most?
5. What advice would you give to a 22-year-old version of yourself?
6. One way to define your character is how others talk about you when you are outside the room.
   - What do you think others would say about you? Perhaps share your thoughts with your team now.
   - How could you find out what others think about you in a safe, non-threatening way?
7. "Nobody cares how much you know until they know how much you care." --Theodore Roosevelt
   - Beyond asking questions of others and active listening, what are some ways other people have shown you they care about you as a person?
   - At work, what are the most meaningful ways people can show you they care about you?
8. "Most people do not listen with the intent to understand; they listen with the intent to reply." --Stephen Covey

Active listening is key rather than while listening, thinking about what you are going to say next.

ENHANCED PARTICIPATION & ENGAGEMENT

1. I am given the support I need to make good decisions at work.
   - What support do you need that you have not always received here in the past?
2. You can't complain about what you permit.
   - Whatever you don't address, you endorse.
3. I know what I need to do to be successful in my role.
   - How do you measure success for yourself?
   - How do we measure success for our team?
4. Do you get to do something at work every day that you love? If so, what is it? If not, what can you do about that?
5. What is one activity that if you could do it every day at work, would most increase your appreciation of your current job?
6. What talent do you have that is not utilized successfully at work?
7. *"If you only read the books that everyone else is reading, you can only think what everyone else is thinking."* —Murakami

Imagine reading a book from an author who has a different view of the world than you do. Imagine having lunch with someone who has different experiences than you, e.g., from a different culture, different nation of origin, different job role.

8. Nothing changes your beliefs faster than experience.
9. Inside all your obstacles are the raw materials to achieve your goals.
10. *"If you don't like something, change it. If you can't change it, change your attitude. Don't complain."* —Maya Angelou

CAREER DEVELOPMENT

1. *"Tell me what you did today, and I'll tell you who you are."* –Mahatma Ghandi
2. *"You can complain or create, but you can't do both at the same time."*–Dennis McIntee
3. What have we learned this week? How will we address this moving forward?
4. What are you most excited about in relation to your job this year?
5. What was the best advice you ever heard?
6. What's the most important thing you have learned in the past year at work?
7. What's one work-related skill you would like to develop this year?
    - Make a list of each team member's response and share the list with your manager—do not include any items which a team member asks not to have included and shared with anyone else.
8. Repetition is the key to mastery.

IMPROVEMENT: Our Company

1. What we do best when onboarding new hires is ____________.
2. What we need to do better when onboarding new hires is _____.
3. What is the single most significant factor, our organization controls, that interferes with our success? ...fuels our success?
4. What request could you make of your manager or senior leader, to improve the company's results?
5. What is something you want the company to do this next year that you've never seen the company do before? (be constructive, professional and mature in your discussion and responses)
6. The culture you create, determines the results you produce.
7. We know what we need to do, so let's stop talking about it and just do it.

IMPROVEMENT: Our Team

1. *"Happiness isn't an outside job, it's an inside job."* –Dennis McIntee
   - Happiness is not to be pursued, it's to be expanded.
2. Most mediocre performance is due to unclear expectations.
   - How do you ask for clarity on expectations for you or your team?
3. See it, Own it, Solve it. -Dennis McIntee
4. What am I currently procrastinating about?
   - And therefore, what I request of you all is ____________.
   - Or, And what I'm going to do about this is ____________.
5. What experience am I providing for my team?

IMPROVEMENT: Our Team

6. Which of these are we the best at, here at work, and which 2 do we need to get better at soon? (focus: our team or department)
   - Clear expectations
   - Allow mistakes—learn from them, and let individual or team address solutions
   - Recognize wins
   - Safety and Health First
   - Don't micromanage
   - Show appreciation often
   - Opportunities to learn something new
   - Make time for fun

7. What's one choice you need to make today to create a different outcome for yourself or the team?
8. How would our daily work experience change if instead of defining people by what they do, we were to focus more on who they are as a person? (e.g., "the housekeeper," "the receptionist," "the sales guy")

Your Patients

CHAPTER 11

Did You Hear Me? Empathic Listening

LISTENING BETTER ON THE PHONE CHECKLIST

These are best practices to help you listen better on the telephone.

- ☐ **Stay focused.** Prevent yourself from being distracted by other staff members or external noises and concentrate on what your caller is saying.
- ☐ **Detect emotions.** Listen to the emotion in your caller's voice. Does it match or endorse the words they are using? Repeat Back With the same Emotions!
- ☐ **Ask questions.** Ask questions to gain more information on points you need to clarify.
- ☐ **Don't interrupt.** You listen more effectively when you're not talking, so refrain from interrupting your caller. Let them finish what they are saying; interruptions may break their train of thought.
- ☐ **Don't pre-empt.** Avoid pre-empting what your caller is going to say, chances are you will be wrong and miss some of the content of their conversation.
- ☐ **Paraphrase key facts.** Paraphrase and reflect back with emotions to check you have heard the key facts and content of the caller's conversation correctly. It also lets the caller know you have understood them. Statements such as "*What I'm hearing is…*" and "*Sounds like you are saying…*" are great ways to reflect back and paraphrase.
- ☐ **Pen and paper handy.** Have a pen and paper on hand and get into the habit of making short quick references to any questions you want to ask or points you wish to raise or comment on. When your caller has finished speaking refer back to your notes and take action. If you are thinking of answers and responses while the caller is speaking, you are not listening.
- ☐ **Say it again.** If you are having difficulty listening, make the necessary adjustments. You might say, "*I'm afraid I missed that last point. Please repeat that for me.*"
- ☐ **Watch the stereotypes.** Avoid stereotyping individuals by making assumptions about how you expect them to act and what you expect them to say. This will bias your listening.

Be aware of the barriers to listening

- We think we're right and the other person is wrong
- We feel we have to provide help right away
- We prefer to talk rather than listen
- We are waiting for gaps or pauses to jump in with our response

CHAPTER 12

The Power of Connecting and Converting Patients Over the Phone

LISTENING BETTER ON THE PHONE CHECKLIST

These are best practices to help you listen better on the telephone.

- ☐ **Stay focused.** Prevent yourself from being distracted by other staff members or external noises and concentrate on what your caller is saying.
- ☐ **Detect emotions.** Listen to the emotion in your caller's voice. Does it match or endorse the words they are using? Repeat Back With the same Emotions!
- ☐ **Ask questions.** Ask questions to gain more information on points you need to clarify.
- ☐ **Don't interrupt.** You listen more effectively when you're not talking, so refrain from interrupting your caller. Let them finish what they are saying; interruptions may break their train of thought.
- ☐ **Don't pre-empt.** Avoid pre-empting what your caller is going to say, chances are you will be wrong and miss some of the content of their conversation.
- ☐ **Paraphrase key facts.** Paraphrase and reflect back with emotions to check you have heard the key facts and content of the caller's conversation correctly. It also lets the caller know you have understood them. Statements such as "*What I'm hearing is...*" and "*Sounds like you are saying...*" are great ways to reflect back and paraphrase.
- ☐ **Pen and paper handy.** Have a pen and paper on hand and get into the habit of making short quick references to any questions you want to ask or points you wish to raise or comment on. When your caller has finished speaking refer back to your notes and take action. If you are thinking of answers and responses while the caller is speaking, you are not listening.
- ☐ **Say it again.** If you are having difficulty listening, make the necessary adjustments. You might say, "*I'm afraid I missed that last point. Please repeat that for me.*"
- ☐ **Watch the stereotypes.** Avoid stereotyping individuals by making assumptions about how you expect them to act and what you expect them to say. This will bias your listening.

Be aware of the barriers to listening

- We think we're right and the other person is wrong
- We feel we have to provide help right away
- We prefer to talk rather than listen
- We are waiting for gaps or pauses to jump in with our response

Connecting and Converting Patient Relationships Checklist

Essential Tools
Empathetic Listening Skills

We can listen for understanding with a "compassionate ear."

Use of Magic Words

With some simple word substitutions, we can not only reduce tension but also build confidence and trust, e.g., yes and; because; thanks; help; invite you to consider; and using their name.

Trust
Trust is built on the foundation of a personal connection.

Training for Success
When training your team, it must be a continual training experience throughout the year, every year. Spaced repetition is the key to results.

"How Do I Get to Your Office?"
If a prospective patient called your office number right now and told your team member, they were new in town and needed directions, what would your team member say? No matter which team member answered the phone, would they consistently be able to ask the patient "From which part of town are you coming?" And then give them directions? Or would they say, "Ma'am, our address 110 Anderson Street comes up on your GPS."

"I Don't Know."
One more great Disney best practice is their corporate edict globally that Cast Members never say "I don't know" to a guest or coworker. Instead, they respond, "That's a great question. Let me find out for you and get right back to you" or, "That's a great question. May I take a moment to find the answer for you?"

Emotional Intelligence
Emotional Intelligence includes awareness (able to identify and name emotions); harnessing emotions (apply emotions to thinking and problem-solving); and, managing emotions (when necessary, adjust your own emotions, or your reaction to others).

Anticipating Patients' Requests
The core guest service standard taught to and expected of every Walt Disney World cast member is, "Consistently Seek Out Guest Contact." The ability to anticipate Patients' requests builds trust, demonstrates sincere care and concern and delights by frequently exceeding their expectations.

Delivering Clear Explanations
The PressGaney Patient Satisfaction Survey and the government's HCAHPS Patient Satisfaction Survey ask Patients whether staff "explain in ways the Patient could understand." Sharing facts and explaining information, procedures, and instructions clearly, slowly, without jargon and at the proper point in the conversation are all important facets of clarifying expectations.

Informing and Educating Patients

Like Treatment Conversations (case acceptance), listening carefully and then informing and/or educating Patients fully creates safety and deepens trust in the relationship. Patients appreciate knowing more after a call than when they first placed the call.

Providing Emotional Support

During phone conversations, strive to listen actively, avoid distractions, do not interrupt, ask for clarification, summarize what you just heard, and provide genuine encouragement, reassurance, and compassion.

Offering Personal Information

Avoid the temptation to share your own experiences/stories in a way that takes the focus off of them, and their experience and feelings at the time. Instead, focus more on listening and asking questions. However, sharing appropriate personal anecdotes quickly does build an emotional connection.

Ensuring Authentic Conversation

Using scripts for calls helps to standardize the intake conversation, the questions asked and the conversation. Sticking to the script is important yet you do not want to sound robotic or mechanical. Instead strive for a balance of genuine conversation and scripted words, phrases, or sentences.

Asking Questions

Questions such as "How are you today?" or "How are you feeling today?" evoke responses that enable you to adapt to the emotional needs of the caller. Clarifying questions ensure you are clearly and fully understanding their needs. Questions create multiple opportunities to emotionally connect with callers.

CHAPTER 13

Case Acceptance: Think Treatment Conversations

Great Discovery Questions for Your Team to Ask New Patients

- Why are you looking for treatment now? Tell me a little bit about your past dental health and how you got to this point?
- What has held you back from getting treatment in the past?
- What will hold you back from getting healthy? Or getting the smile you have always wanted?
- Have you ever had an amazing experience at a dental practice? Please share what made it amazing for you.
- Poor experience? Please share what made it poor for you.
- If we can give you what you want, make dentistry affordable, and fit a budget you are comfortable with, would you be interested in moving forward?

Keys to Successful Treatment Conversations:

- Take calls OFF the front desk (truly listen without disruption)
- Hire the right team members (*Hire Happy...Train for Skill*)
- Practice high emotional intelligence amongst your entire team
- Use empathic listening skills consistently
- Train team on the use of "Magic Words" from Tim David's book, The Science and Secrets Behind Seven Words That Motivate, Engage, and Influence
- Know and avoid the Three Pitfalls to Failure when scheduling a patient
- Ask great discovery questions (see below)
- ABC (Always Be Converting)
- Record calls, listen, evaluate calls--provide timely coaching (sooner the better)

CHAPTER 14

Achieving Service Excellence: Fostering a Culture of Quality Outcomes

What is the Disney Difference?
(excerpt chapter from *Success from the Inside Out* by Steven Rowell)

Leveraging Disney Principles within Your Own Program

Ever since leaving the employment of The Walt Disney World Co., I have been asked so many times, "What is the Disney Difference?" or "What makes Disney so successful?" The three areas that people are most intrigued by or interested in, are 1) understanding the secrets to Disney's overall success—organizationally, branding, as an employer; 2) understanding the secrets to Disney leadership principles that make a difference; 3) what it is like to be a Cast Member working for Disney. More recently there has been a fascination with Disney from the health care industry to understand and then leverage Disney principles to achieve greater patient satisfaction.

Here I will share, for the very first time, an insider's look into the principles that guide Disney's success. I am offering only those practices and principles which I believe are relevant for you to consider and reflect upon when you are strategizing your own next steps as a Leader, especially in this industry. I invite you to consider adopting and adapting any of these principles within your own Leadership practice.

Disney's Enduring Principles

- We Sell Happiness (capture your essence in five words or less)
- Safety, Courtesy, Show, Efficiency (Four guiding principles, the order does matter, they build upon the previous principle—this is one of the most enduring, unique aspects of Disney because the vision is "complete" encompassing the total process and experience for a Cast Member and a Guest) **UPDATE 2023 Now there are 5—Safety, Courtesy, Inclusion, Show, Efficiency.
- Walt Disney was a master storyteller. Story telling is at the core of all Disney does today—whether its new hire orientation, training a new hire, welcoming Guests to a theme park, Guests entering an attraction, or even having dinner at a Disney Resort
- High-touch refers to building interaction into the Guest experience, giving Guests the chance to participate, make choices and interact with the Cast; High-show refers to the need to build vivid presentations that are memorable into the Guest experience; High- tech refers to the need to build speed, accuracy, and expertise into your service delivery which results in giving your Guests the gift

of time and cutting edge products and services—the creation of FastPass and the ticketing system used at Disney theme parks are examples of high-tech **UPDATE FastPass is no longer in use.

- Your Organization is only as good as your selection process—Hire for attitude, Train for Skill is their focus—Quality begins in the recruitment/selection process rather than in the training process—Disney hires people who are already courteous, positive, enthusiastic and people-oriented rather than waste millions of dollars on teaching people "how to be nice" or "how to smile"
- Brilliantly in the mid-1990's, they redefined career success as laterally transferring and taking on multiple roles over time as more valuable than simply being promoted vertically—this was brilliant for retention, Cast Member satisfaction, retaining organizational history by retaining veteran Cast Members and minimizing the pressure to grow in terms of attractions and resorts in order to retain "A" Talent Cast Members

Every Guest matters, no matter what

- Always, always, always, *see the world through the eyes of your Guests*—make changes immediately if you discover something wrong
- Continually look for barriers to achieving service excellence—identify the barriers and then eliminate them, period
- Guidelines for Guest Service include Make Eye Contact and Smile!, Greet and Welcome

Each and Every Guest, Seek Out Guest Contact, Provide Immediate Service Recovery, Display Appropriate Body Language at All Times, Preserve the "Magical" Guest Experience, and Thank Each and Every Guest

- ***Everything Speaks*** means even the smallest details matter—it is in the mastery of the smaller details along with the major details that makes it possible for an organization, a team or an individual to achieve truly legendary service. Some examples of this are, 1) appropriate, accurate, adequate signage; 2) what does your parking garage look like to your customers?; 3) elevator buttons that are mislabeled and never updated; 4) phone directories that are not kept current; 5) failing to minimize clutter and personal trash within a work area that is visible by guests; 6) employees using language that is most appropriate at all times.
- ***Living our Culture*** every day is what makes the place magical—the service we provide within our Culture is what is expected by our Guests
- Disney Service is rooted in the magic of show business—everyone performs a role for the Guests and creating magical memories from the Show for Guests is the Cast Member's ultimate responsibility
- **Language Matters**—It is critically important to the culture o Hotels are called *Resorts* o Rides are called *Attractions* o Customers are called *Guests* o Employees are called *Cast Members* o Managers are called *Coaches* o You are either *On-stage* or *Back-stage* o Buses are *Motor Coaches*
- Cast Members are *Hosts* when speaking with a Guest, e.g., Security Guard is *Security Host*; Bus Driver is *Motor Coach Host*; "Ride Operators" are Attractions Hosts

Disney Best Practices

The Disney Casting Center's use of a **8-minute preview video** with all applicants that helps describe the nature of a day working at Disney—on average 10-13% of all Job Fair respondents leave the process immediately after the first step of reviewing this video— great best practice to eliminate wrong-fit talent at the beginning of the selection process.

- New Hire Orientation known as **Traditions**, is facilitated by front-line, hourly paid Cast Members who serve as Traditions Assistants as a cross-utilization role—meaning they maintain their full-time or part-time position within the company and serve periodically as a ***Traditions Assistant***

- **Trash cans**, on stage, are positioned no more than 19 paces apart because of the research Disney conducted in the mid-1980's when they discovered the average Guest would drop a piece of trash on the ground after 19 paces, if a trash can was not readily available

- **Tele-Cast**: A tri-fold, double-sided, pocket-sized information card which lists all relevant show times, theme park hours, telephone numbers, Guest information, and unique information relevant to "this week" which is most useful in assisting Cast Members who are attempting to answer Guests' questions on-stage.

- **Costuming and Disney Look Book** (grooming guidelines) along with the use of backstage Mirrors placed in key Cast Member areas close to doors that are leading onto onstage areas—these mirrors are 3 ft. by 5 ft., large enough to catch your attention as you are walking by. This powerfully reinforces how serious the organization is always for everyone to look their best. Hospitals and hotels have implemented this with great success. Examples of Disney grooming are, men on-stage cannot have hair that touches their collar, women must wear only natural tones of eye shadow, no mascara, and earrings smaller than a quarter with no hoop earrings allowed at all, one ring per hand, and no tattoos can be visible in costume for on-stage Cast Members male or female.

- **Telephone scripting**—commitment to every Cast Member saying to every Guest on the telephone, just before ending the conversation, "*Have a Magical Day.*" It wasn't until 3 years of consistent success with this property-wide that management began to allow evening shift Cast Members say "*Have a Magical Evening*" or "*Have a Magical Night.*" Consistency in the execution of best practices, is at the heart of Disney's Magic and Success.

- **Navigational Directions** are available at every telephone either onstage (such as a front desk of a hotel) or backstage throughout the property—this facilitates the Cast Members' ability to provide directions to Guests or fellow Cast Members WITHOUT transferring the call or passing the burden of finding directions onto someone else. Again, Cast Members own the Guest's experience and they treat fellow Cast Members as their own Guests.

- **Magic Towelfolding** is a surprise found in Disney resort rooms, by Guests returning to their room after a day at the theme parks. This has become one of the most frequently commented items in Guest Letters. See the Service Special Report #1 Creative Towel Folding for examples.

Disney Leaders Truly Do It Differently:

- Disney Leaders ACTUALLY can perform the roles of their subordinates, this comes from Disney's philosophy that their managers are competent in the roles for which they are responsible, as well as the Disney's exceptionally high percentage of leader positions which are filled from internal promotion

- Hands-on leadership, with constant walking around, with eyes wide open from the perspective of what the Guest sees is the standard for all Leaders
- Never eat, drink, smoke, or chew gum on stage (in guest areas), even if there is no one around
- Never carry drinks, food, cigarettes or chewing gum on stage—none of this ever in shirt, jacket or pants pockets while on stage
- Never turn your back to a Guest when you are on stage—they even now embroider the name of the Cast Member on the back of their lanyard (positioned on the back of the neck) so that Guests walking up onto the Cast Member from behind can use the Cast Members name immediately
- Never conduct a personal conversation with another Cast Member on stage regardless of whether there are Guests within listening distance or not
- Pick up clutter as soon as you see it—this is so that the next Guest never sees the clutter—this is true for every Cast Member from front-line through senior vice presidents, and is modeled frequently by all
- Personal accountability and the managerial courage required to achieve it are honored, expected, trained, modeled and lived by Leaders (not by all, but by a vast majority)
- When Disney Leaders leave Disney property for a meal or errands on personal time, they immediately remove their Disney name tag (in contrast, think about how many people you see sitting at lunch wearing their name tags at a restaurant near your workplace—sometimes I have fun with these people by walking up, saying hello and announcing their name—they can't figure out why I know their name or why they can't seem to remember who I am)
- As a Leader, you are PART of the Show, you are NOT the Show
- Disney Leaders OWN the experience of their Cast Members because Cast Members are the Leader's Guests (Every Cast Member is a future potential Disney Guest)
- At company functions, a Disney Leader wearing a Disney name tag will never be seen posing for a photograph with an alcoholic beverage in hand
- Disney Leaders own the training of their subordinates—this is not delegated to trainers or others, except in the case of new hire orientation known as Traditions, and scheduled management development programs that are company-wide initiatives
- Give your employees the tools they need to deliver exceptional service or perform exceptional work—simple examples, 1) driving directions to your facility posted at every telephone; 2) pocket guides with all of the most important need-to-know information for employees to share with

Guests; 3) backstage mirrors mounted on the wall so employees can check themselves one last time before they go out "on stage"

- As a Disney Leader you are only successful when your people are successful. Your role as Leader is to develop your staff while maintaining the Show and providing the services required for your Guests

- Take 5: Commitment on the part of managers to "Take 5" minutes with a minimum number of their Cast Members each day at work. The focus of "Take 5" conversations is to check in with the Cast Member on how things are going and listen for feedback or concerns. This practice directly impacts employee satisfaction long-term.

Disney's Great Leader Strategies
(Introduced in the 1990's as the Standard for Great Leaders)

1. Design your organizational structure for success…break the mold.
2. Make sure you have the right people in the right job.
3. Ensure team members are knowledgeable about their jobs.
4. Make dramatic leaps in quality work and quality service.
5. Implement effective structured processes for getting work done.
6. Explore, probe and know what is going on in your organization and act upon the information.
7. Actively observe and react to the performance of your direct reports—take time for recognition, coaching and counseling.
8. Expand and act upon knowledge and experience of the best service available anywhere.
9. Partner effectively and successfully with staff and other cross-functional partners.
10. Demonstrate a passionate, professional commitment to your job.

The Bottom-Line

The culture of the Disney organization is a bundling of Show Business, Everything Speaks, "We Sell Happiness," Guests and Cast Members, "we're only as good as our hiring," Change is Constant, Creating Magical Memories is what it's all about, and Safety, Courtesy, Inclusion, Show and Efficiency lead to Exceeding Guests' Expectations.

The reality is that culture will beat strategy every time when it comes to organizations trying to implement new strategies or techniques mid-stream (any time after the inception of the organization). Therefore, organizations must affect change at the level of culture change, rather than simply implementing service excellence strategies, or best practices.

In other words, Disney theme parks are so clean, and the Cast Members are so friendly and service oriented, because the established, proven, tested culture expects:

- Cast Members to be hired that already demonstrate the "friendly" and "service oriented" attitude during the interview process
- We are in Show Business, we all have a role to perform for our audience of Guests

- Each Cast Member has the opportunity, moment-to-moment, to either support the Disney culture or not honor it—and supporting the culture is rewarded, recognized and expected in hundreds of ways, such as; Cast Members bend over and pick up clutter as soon as they see it onstage; kneel down on one knee when addressing a child; children are never lost, their parents are; or Cast Members are to take no part in eating, drinking, smoking or chewing gum on stage.
- *We are each a part of the Show* which is something that has tremendous power and meaning within it and is a purpose larger than ourselves. Therefore, to be a part of it, no matter how minor the role, is to cherish the awesome responsibility we each must live the Magic
- The culture is so strong, so real, so current, and so ever-present that execution and performance are not just expected, it is *our way of life at Disney.*

The million-dollar challenge is to facilitate culture change and redefine effective leadership within an organization that has failed to achieve Disney's level of quality work and service focus and culture since its inception. This is the critical challenge for any organization to move from Marginal to Good, and Good to Exceptional. Language and storytelling are the two most powerful tools to building a lasting organizational culture. *Disney Institute* has published several books on the secrets to the *Disney Magic.*

Service Excellence Internal Assessment and Checklist

- ☐ Do you have a customer service policy in place?
- ☐ Is your staff properly trained in customer service?
- ☐ Are your staff members friendly and welcoming?
- ☐ Are you providing a comfortable waiting room? Are you leveraging technology here?
- ☐ Do you have an efficient check-in process?
- ☐ Is there clear communication between you and your patients?
- ☐ Are you offering convenient payment options?
- ☐ Are you keeping patient records up-to-date?
- ☐ Are you offering follow-up care after appointments?
- ☐ Are you responding promptly to phone calls/emails from patients?
- ☐ Are you staying up-to-date on industry trends/best practices?
- ☐ Do you offer any loyalty programs/discounts/rewards programs for returning customers?
- ☐ Do you provide educational materials/resources related to dental health/procedures?
- ☐ Do you offer any other services outside of dental care (e..g., teeth whitening)?
- ☐ Do all of your staff members wear name tags while working with patients?
- ☐ Do all employees greet guests upon arrival at the office?
- ☐ Do all employees thank guests upon departure from the office?
- ☐ Do you greet each patient with a warm and friendly smile?
- ☐ Are all staff members trained to be knowledgeable about dental procedures, insurance plans, and payment options?
- ☐ Is there a system in place for handling patient complaints or concerns in a timely manner?
- ☐ Are patients provided with clear instructions about how to care for their teeth at home?
- ☐ Does the practice offer flexible appointment times to accommodate schedules?
- ☐ Does the practice use modern technology such as digital x-rays or electronic health records (EHRs)?
- ☐ Are there opportunities for feedback from patients regarding their experience at the practice?
- ☐ Are the receptionists courteous and professional when answering the phone and greeting patients?
- ☐ Is there an efficient process in place for scheduling appointments?
- ☐ Is there an effective system in place for following up with patients after their appointment?
- ☐ Are employees trained regularly on best practices related to customer ?
- ☐ Do employees receive regular feedback from management about their performance related to customer service?
- ☐ Does the office provide information about treatments available at the practice clearly before scheduling appointments?
- ☐ Are patients informed about their treatment options before beginning any procedure?
- ☐ Are patient concerns addressed promptly by knowledgeable staff?

CHAPTER 15

Discover the Benefits of Implant Dentistry

There are no additional resources for this chapter.

Your Practice

CHAPTER 16

Employee Engagement: The Key to Success

Reality Check: The Positives and Challenges of Dentistry & What to Do About It

Positives

Good Income: This career provides a stable income and there is potential to make a significant income. This isn't easy money though. This job can be extremely challenging with a lot to learn after dental school about running a business. But the rewards from helping people transform their smile and their health are even greater than the income.

Respect: The profession of dentistry is well respected and held in high esteem by the general public.

Independence: As an owner of your own business, you are free to make the decisions, yet you also take on the risk. But the freedom provided by entrepreneurship is rewarding for those so inclined.

Caring for People: Similar to other healthcare professions, dentistry is foremost about helping people with their health. The relationships you build with your patients and your team members can last a lifetime.

Adrenaline: There is plenty of excitement in the job of a dentist. You get to juggle lots of things at once, and throughout the workday. It is far better than a desk job for sure.

Interesting: Every day is different…different patients and different procedures. There is always the opportunity to learn something new, and to challenge the status quo.

Schedule: Flexibility in the hours worked is a definite strong suit for dentists. You can build your life schedule almost any way you want. Part-time, full-time, weekends, mornings only, or afternoons and evenings. Some dentists only work from 12pm to 7pm every weekday.

Meaningful Work: You help people maintain their smile, or regain their smile, and you directly improve their health through your work as well.

Practical Work: The work you do provides tangible immediate benefit to your patients. You get to improve the lives of your patients in meaningful ways.

Art and Science: Dentistry allows you to immerse yourself in the medicine and science of dentistry, while also experiencing the artistry of implant and cosmetic dentistry.

Job Security: People will always need help with their teeth and gums. Patients start with dentistry as a young child, and visit dentists the rest of their lives.

Challenges

Investment: You can expect to have sizable student loan debt from $100k to $500k.

Schooling: Including college, you can expect at least 12 years of your life to complete the required schooling to become a dentist.

Costs: To start your own practice it can takes hundreds of thousands of dollars, even up to a couple million dollars, especially if you are building a new practice from the ground up (de novo). There is continuing education required every year as well. And if not managed well, there can be high overhead in running your own practice.

Serious Responsibility: The buck stops with you as they say. Whether it is administering anesthesia, conducting surgery, or prescribing medications, these are all serious significant responsibilities in helping your patients.

Burnout: Dentistry is a stressful job with as many as 20 different stressors commonly found in the daily life of a dentist. Long hours, working in tight cramped spaces for long periods of time, and following a rigorous time schedule every day require a person to have a high level of resilience and adaptability.

Tough Patients: Some patients are never satisfied no matter what you do or offer them. Some clinical procedures turn out to be especially difficult.

Being Despised: No one likes to be hated, yet dentists must endure the reality that many of their patients vehemently don't want to be there, and many are filled with fear during the entire appointment.

Intensity: Lots can happen on any given day. While this can be exciting and adrenaline pumping, it can also be exhausting. Due to the tight spaces of working inside someone's mouth, patient after patient, day after day, the job can be surprisingly intense yet monotonous too.

Physical Stress: Spending long hours hunched over working in tiny spaces takes a toll on your body after years of doing this day-in and day-out.

Unpleasant Moments: Even for the most clinically-minded dentist, the condition of a person's mouth sometimes can be disconcerting or even gross.

Insurance: Dealing with dental insurances can be stressful for patients and dentists. So much so, many seasoned dentists stop accepting dental insurance altogether.

Your Team Culture Blueprint

This is the outline of the Senior Leader presentation that communicates your values and your culture to all team members. This type of presentation should be made at least once a year, and a version of it can be recorded and used in new hire orientation as well.

Premise of Senior Leader Presentation Version
The opportunity here is for a Senior Leader to "humanize" themselves for their team's sake for the following reasons:

- Learn a little bit about you, your values, and your definition of excellence
- Build trust with your team when they learn more about you and your expectations of them
- Builds confidence in your informal group leaders amongst your team, and your top performing team members who already champion you and your mission, to speak up and reinforce your message, after the meeting, with any team members who may be negative or "not on the bus"
- Employee engagement and loyalty will increase for many of your team members in response to your sharing
- Stress reduction for team members of all types due to the clarification of your personal story; values; beliefs; definition of excellence; definition of success; and expectations

Talking Points
For each of the following categories, **choose 3 or 4 most important to you, and/or most important messages** you want your team members to hear right now, i.e., Personal Story; Values; Beliefs; Definition of Excellence; Definition of Success; Expectations; What You the Senior Leader Are Willing to Do.

Less is More...share what you think will have the greatest impact in terms of your team understanding each category. This should probably take you 15 to 20 minutes to present, depending upon how many stories you wish to tell along the way. Using presentation slides for each category with your bulleted lists is recommended, especially for your visual learners on your team.

THE FOLLOWING ARE EXAMPLES OF POSSIBLE TALKING POINTS...JUST EXAMPLES...IT IS IMPORTANT TO MAKE THESE LISTS YOUR OWN WITH YOUR OWN LANGUAGE.
For each of these topics, pick the 3-4 talking points **of your own** that are most important and relatable to your team members.

Personal Story (Examples)

- Short version (however vulnerable you wish to be)
- Growing up I always dreamed of becoming an Astronaut because...but then I had xyz experience and that changed everything
- My father teaching me the value of hard work and dedication
- Discovering a Mentor from...who helped me...
- One big life lesson I learned while growing up—youth, high school, college
- One failure in my life and the lessons I learned from it (your team will learn far more from your failures and lessons learned, than from your success stories—and **they will trust you more** as well)

My Values (Examples)

- Be Generous in All Aspects of Life
- Always Moving Forward…Never Standing Still
- Always Competing Against Myself…Wanting to Be Better Than Yesterday
- Humility…I am Willing to Do Whatever It Takes
- No Ego…I Can Learn Something from Anyone…Always Strive to Stay Humble
- Not Afraid to Fail…Mistakes and Failure are Experience and Lessons

My Beliefs (Examples)

- New Clients/Patients Deserve a Wow Experience
- Your Success is Not What You Do, It is How You Do It
- Success in This Business is Based on…
- Treating Your Employees Well and Compensating Them is Important
- I Enjoy Mentoring Team Members Who Want to Learn and Grow, and Consistently Demonstrate Hard Work and Hustle
- Lead Teams, Don't Manage Them

Our Definition of Excellence (Examples)

- Our Clients Experience Consistent High Quality of Service
- Our Team Members Anticipate Our Clients' Needs
- No Such Thing as "I Don't Know" in Response to Clients' Questions
- Excellence is Defined by Our Own Standards, AND by Our Clients' Perception

Our Definition of Success (Examples)

- Our Team Members Feel Respected, Honored and Safe at Work Always
- Team Members Do Not Gossip
- Assuming the Best First and We Don't Avoid Difficult Conversations
- Our Clients Become Raving Fans Because of the Services We Provide
- At Least 30% of Our New Clients are Referred to Us by Our Own Clients
- We Meet if Not Exceed Financial Targets so We Stay in Business and Grow

My Expectations of Myself and You, Our Team Members (Examples)

- Take Responsibility for Your Choices, Actions, Results and Impact on Others
- Strive to Learn and Improve…Do Not Just Settle and Become Complacent
- Be Humble, Open to Feedback and Coaching
- Always Focus on Moving Forward and Making Things Better
- Speak Up: When You See Something Say Something
- Choose to Be Positive at Work…Leave Drama at Home
- Always Strive for Providing a Wow Client Experience

What I (CEO/Senior Leader) am Willing to Do in Support of You and Your Teams (Examples)

- Frequently Ask Questions to Better Understand Your Work Experience
- Solicit Your Input and Suggestions More Often and Provide Timely Feedback
- Meet Monthly to Discuss What is Working Well and What is Not Working
- Support You with Training Opportunities Whenever Possible
- Meet with You Quarterly One-on-One to Discuss Your Progress

Wrap Up at End of Presentation

After Senior Leader shares this presentation, one of the most powerful, effective, and efficient ways to wrap this up is to simply ask your team members to pair up in small groups of 2 or 3 people, and simply share with one another what they heard you just share...what stood out to them, what was most important, what are they grateful for, etc. Give them 3 to 5 minutes for this discussion. Then bring them back and invite anyone to ask clarifying questions. Focusing on clarifying questions is best, rather than just asking for questions. You want this portion of your meeting to end on a positive note.

CHAPTER 17

Strengthening Your Leadership and Executive Teams

Stop, Start, Continue Feedback Exercise

Two of the more powerful and effective tools I share with my clients for them to use in facilitating team meetings and individual meetings as well are, Stop, Start, Continue and Mad, Glad and Sad.

Some of the most common situations to use these tools in are:

- Teambuilding with staff or management teams
- Soliciting feedback from front-line staff
- Facilitating constructive coaching conversations with an individual
- Discussions with almost anyone when your need is to discover the "real issues" of a situation or a relationship

Stop, Start, Continue and Mad, Glad and Sad can be completed in private by groups of individuals, in dialogue with an individual, or as an interactive team exercise for an entire team simultaneously (using flipcharts for data capture).

A traditional example of using Stop, Start, Continue with a group of employees, is to pass one copy of the Stop, Start, Continue form to each participant. Then ask everyone to quietly, with no discussion, read through the handout and then ask them to write down their responses to the following questions privately using the Stop, Start, Continue handout.

You could then facilitate a group discussion, asking individual participants to share whatever they are comfortable sharing in discussion with the entire group.

This Stop, Start, Continue form can be used with individuals in private one-on-one conversations as well in an effort to offer a tool to guide your discussion. You could send the form to the person in advance of your meeting as well if this makes your face-to-face time more meaningful and efficient.

Another method of using this Stop, Start, Continue process is to bring a group of 10-12 employees or managers together (traditionally this is not used with managers and staff in the same group—at least in the beginning of your use of this process). Using flipcharts around the room, one labeled STOP, one labeled START and one labeled CONTINUE, you simply ask everyone to either approach the flip chart pages and write their ideas down under each category, or use post it notes first—with one idea written per post-it, and then ask the participants to place their post-its on the flipchart pages under each category.

There are advantages and disadvantages to each of these data collection methods for Stop, Start, Continue (or Mad, Glad and Sad).

Method One—asking participants to use markers and write their ideas under each Category, STOP, START, CONTINUE.

ADVANTAGES:

- Participants are able to move around the room at their own will
- Participants are able to write down their own thoughts without having to share with the larger group
- Data collection tends to be extremely fast due to the fact that people disburse throughout the room—this is especially true for larger groups when you post multiple blank flipchart pages on the walls for each category, STOP, START, CONTINUE
- Flipchart pages can be easily stored for use later in typing up the data from the meeting

DISADVANTAGES:

- Participants tend to watch people as they write their comments down on the flipchart pages which can prove challenging or anxiety provoking for some participants—this contributes to the possibility for group think to occur as well—that is, participants to change their responses after seeing what others have begun to write on the various flipcharts—to an extreme, participants becoming biased by the presence of one or two comments and then these participants simply following along with these few statements rather than contributing what they are truly feeling or needing to express.

Method Two—asking participants to use POST-IT Notes, one post-it per idea, and then participants place each of their POST-IT Notes under each Category, STOP, START, CONTINUE.

ADVANTAGES:

- Participants perceive greater privacy, because they fill out each POST-IT note in the room with the group, but without letting anyone see what they are writing
- Participants get out of their seats to place their POST-IT notes, but again, most participants cannot see what is written on other people's POST-IT notes during this process
- The use of POST-IT notes allows you or the facilitator to organize the POST- IT notes quickly under each category in themes, or to consolidate repetitious comments
- Repetitious comments can be easily organized by placing POST-IT notes together in a line for each category, which visually shows the frequency of comments for each theme under each category. Some of my clients put the POST-IT notes in columns or rows in order to show the frequencies of each issues, resulting in a bar graph of POST-IT notes or a histogram.

DISADVANTAGES:

- Once the POST-IT notes are put on the flipchart pages, they are difficult to be read by participants once everyone is back in their seats for discussion— the handwriting tends to be small.
- After the meeting, the handling of the flipchart pages is a little more tedious because the POST-IT notes can tend to fall off or move as the flipchart pages are folded and utilized later

Once your team's data is collected, you can use a variety of methods to have your team prioritize the various themes or ideas under each category, STOP, START and CONTINUE.

A similar process is used to solicit feedback using Mad, Glad and Sad. The best method is to conduct Mad, Glad and Sad exercise first. Then conduct the *Stop, Start, Continue* exercise.

Examples of questions to use in the use of Stop, Start, Continue are:

- What could we Stop, Start or Continue to do together as a department, to make this a better place to work?
- What could I Stop, Start or Continue to do as your boss, to become an even better boss?
- What do each of us need to Stop, Start or Continue doing in order to become more effective team members?
- Thinking of the way in which this team communicates on a regular basis, what do we need to Stop, Start or Continue doing?

Examples of questions to use in the use of Mad, Glad and Sad are:

- Thinking of your daily work life here at work, what are you Mad about, Glad about, and Sad about?
- When you think of how our team interacts and supports each other, what are you Mad about, Glad about and Sad about?
- When you think of how we treat our customers or patients, what are you Mad about, Glad about and Sad about?

The only "rules" to use when soliciting feedback from participants using these two tools:

- If you provide an idea under one category, please offer another idea under one of the other categories—e.g., if you list a Stop, list a Start too; if you list a Mad, list a Glad too.
- Your contribution must be genuine, constructive and sensitively worded.

Confidential Version

If confidentiality is critically important (especially the first time you conduct this feedback exercise) you may prefer to use this confidential method of collecting participants' feedback data.

Provide everyone a single piece of 8.5 x 11 paper, a pen, and an "interoffice-type envelope." For both Mad, Glad and Sad, and Stop, Start and Continue, ask each participant to privately write down their thoughts under each category, e.g., Mad, Glad, Sad, on one side of the paper. Then use the other side of the paper for

Stop, Start, Continue. Once each participant is finished, they may put their own paper, and only their paper, into their envelope. Then they simply pass their closed envelopes forward.

Using this method, typically the data is collected in the envelopes, and the data is compiled confidentially and then reported back to all participants.

Examples of How to Frame the Questions
The following examples simply demonstrate how to ask the questions as they related to a specific topic or issue.

These feedback exercises are routinely used to solicit feedback from team members in the following areas:

- Teamwork and communication between departments and/or team members
- Improving the Patient experience
- Increasing Accountability amongst the team
- Leaders asking for feedback about how they can better support their team
- Improving processes, systems or methods within the business, e.g., ordering supplies; following up with former Patients
- Improving safety procedures, policies and practices
- Identifying cost savings or ways to sell more services and/or products

Obviously, you may have other topics as well.

Here is an example of how to modify the questions to fit each topic:

"When you think about the past 6 months, and how we have been ordering supplies, what are you Mad about, Sad about and Glad about?"

Then conduct the Stop, Start and Continue version using this question.

"Thinking of the current Patient experience we provide our Patients, what are you Mad, Glad and Sad about?"
Then, Stop, Start and Continue.

"When you think about teamwork, communication amongst team members/departments, and accountability, what are you Mad, Sad and Glad about?"

You can do each item separately if you wish, e.g., teamwork and they write down their thoughts; then you ask about communication, and they write; and then you ask about accountability. This usually creates more clear data in terms of their comments and connecting them with the correct topic.

- What am I GLAD about?
- What are my priorities to address?
- What Should We START doing?
- What Should We CONTINUE doing?
- What are the BENEFITS to us, our Patients, and others?

CURRENT CONCERNS:

What am I MAD about?

What am I SAD about?

What am I GLAD about?

What are my priorities to address?

PERSONAL COMMITMENTS:

What Should I STOP doing?

What Should I START doing?

What Should I CONTINUE doing?

What are the BENEFITS to me?

Management versus Leadership Self-Assessment

Dental practice owners serve in both roles, as a manager, and as a leader. The question is whether you are only a manager, or a manager who can truly lead people.

A manager is responsible for planning and decision making (determining a course of action); organizing (coordinating activities and resources); controlling (monitoring and evaluating activities).

A leader is values-driven, influential, collaborative and purposeful. Leaders ask questions, inspire enthusiasm, earn respect, make employees feel valued, trust employees will perform their jobs well, and develop, coach, and mentor employees.

Reflect on each of these questions and whether you spend more time at work as a manager, or as a leader. Also make note of areas you can improve your role as a leader.

How often do I encourage my team to take initiative and come up with creative solutions?
A leader understands innovation is key in the dental practice, and they are always looking for ways to improve processes and procedures. A manager, on the other hand, may be more focused on following established protocols and may not be open to change or new ideas.

Do I foster an environment of collaboration among my staff?
Leaders create an environment where collaboration is encouraged among staff members. They understand that different perspectives can lead to better decisions, so they create opportunities for team members to work together and share ideas. They recognize collaboration is essential for success and will actively seek out opportunities for their teams to work together on projects or initiatives. Managers, however, may be more focused on individual tasks and may not prioritize collaboration as much as a leader would.

How often do I provide feedback to my staff?
Leaders provide feedback to their staff on a regular basis in order to help them grow professionally. They recognize that feedback can be a powerful tool for motivating employees and helping them reach their goals. Managers, however, may not prioritize giving feedback as much as leaders do, which can lead to an unengaged workforce.

Do I delegate tasks appropriately?
Leaders delegate tasks appropriately in order to ensure that each team member is given the opportunity to use their skills effectively and contribute meaningfully to the dental practice's success. Leaders go beyond simply assigning tasks; they also provide guidance, feedback, and resources so that employees can complete their assignments successfully. Managers may not delegate tasks as effectively because they are more focused on controlling every aspect of the business instead of empowering others within it.

How often do I hold meetings with my staff?
Leaders hold regular meetings with their staff in order to stay informed about what is going on in the practice and ensure everyone is working towards common goals. Managers may not prioritize communication as much as leaders do, which can lead to confusion and miscommunication among staff members.

Do I take the time to understand my team's individual goals and motivations?

As a leader, it is important to take the time to understand each member of your team's individual goals and motivations. This helps you better identify how you can support them in achieving their objectives and encourages them to be more productive and engaged in their work. As a manager, however, you may be more focused on tasks and results than understanding your team's individual needs.

Do I provide clear direction for my team?

Leaders are able to provide clear direction for their teams by setting expectations, providing feedback, and offering guidance when needed. This helps create an environment where everyone knows what is expected of them and how they can contribute to achieving the team's goals. Managers, on the other hand, may not always provide clear direction or offer guidance which can lead to confusion among team members.

Do I empower my team members to make decisions?

Leaders understand that empowering their teams leads to greater engagement from employees which leads to increased productivity and improved performance overall. They will give their teams autonomy over decision-making so they feel empowered to make choices without fear of repercussions or criticism from management. Managers may be less likely to do this as they prefer having control over all aspects of operations. Managers tend not to prioritize giving decision-making authority away since it requires additional effort on their part.

Do I celebrate successes with my team?

Leaders understand the importance of celebrating successes with their teams as it helps foster a sense of accomplishment and motivates employees to continue striving for excellence in their work. Managers may not take the time to recognize successes or acknowledge accomplishments due to being too focused on completing tasks quickly rather than taking a moment to appreciate what has been achieved by the team collectively or individually.

Do I create an environment that encourages open communication among team members?

As a manager, it is important to foster an environment in which team members feel comfortable communicating their ideas and opinions and working together to achieve the practice's goals. Leaders create this type of environment by encouraging dialogue, actively listening to team members, and providing support and resources for employees to succeed.

Do I take the time to mentor my staff?

Managers may be focused on getting tasks completed quickly and efficiently; however, leaders understand the importance of taking time out of their day to invest in their staff by providing mentorship opportunities. Mentoring allows leaders to share their knowledge with others and help them grow professionally.

Am I open-minded when it comes to new ideas or approaches?

Leaders are open-minded when it comes to considering new ideas or approaches that may improve the dental practice's operations or processes. Managers may be more resistant to change if they perceive it as a risk or as something that could disrupt existing systems or procedures.

Do I recognize the accomplishments of my team members?

Leaders recognize the hard work and dedication of their team members by offering praise for successful projects or initiatives. Managers may not take the time out of their day-to-day operations to thank employees for their efforts; however, doing so can help foster a positive work environment and motivate employees to do their best work each day.

Do I encourage creativity among my staff?
Leaders understand that creativity is essential for innovation within any organization; therefore, they strive to create an atmosphere where creativity is encouraged among all team members regardless of position or seniority level. Managers may not prioritize creative thinking as much as leaders do because they focus more on completing tasks quickly than on exploring new possibilities or solutions.

Do I take responsibility when things don't go according to plan?
Leaders accept responsibility when things don't go according to plan instead of placing blame on individual team members or external factors beyond anyone's control; managers may be more likely than leaders are to assign blame rather than accept responsibility for mistakes made within the dental practice's operations or processes.

Do I show appreciation for everyone's contributions?
Leaders value every contribution made by each member of the dental practice's staff; even small gestures such as thanking someone for helping with a task can have a big impact on morale in the workplace over time. Managers may overlook these types of contributions since they are focused primarily on completing tasks efficiently rather than recognizing individual efforts.

Am I willing to make difficult decisions when necessary?
Leaders understand that difficult decisions must sometimes be made in order for a dental practice's operations run smoothly; managers may avoid making these types of decisions out of fear that they could negatively affect employee morale or lead to conflict within the workplace.

CHAPTER 18

Work Less. Earn More. Change Lives. ™

Costly Mistakes to Avoid in Growing Your Dental Practice Checklist

- ☐ **Failing to research the local market** before opening additional locations. It is important to consider local competition, population density, median income and community health initiatives when selecting a new site.
- ☐ **Underinvesting in marketing activities.** It is essential for any business to invest in marketing activities such as creating ads for local publications, social media and television, partnering with charities or sponsorships of local events to build awareness of the practice location. Also remember it is the conversion rate of your marketing that matters most, and don't forget to split test your ads, especially online.
- ☐ **Not setting up a customer relationship management system.** A dental practice should invest in a CRM that is designed to manage appointments, patient records, and billing information. This system will improve the efficiency and accuracy of the practice's operations.
- ☐ **Not investing in technology.** Investing in digital tools such as electronic medical records, X-ray machines, and other state-of-the-art equipment will provide better patient care.
- ☐ **Ignoring compliance regulations.** It is crucial to keep up with healthcare regulations by monitoring regularly changing laws and updating policies to meet the requirements. Failure to do so can result in hefty fines or legal issues that could damage the practice's reputation.
- ☐ **Not tracking performance metrics.** Without these measurements, the practice will fail to measure its success or make necessary changes in order to stay profitable.
- ☐ **Not providing competitive salaries or benefits.** Salaries and benefits are key factors in attraction, retention and employee satisfaction and the success of any business.
- ☐ **Not offering follow-up care.** In addition to a quality patient experience, offering post-treatment follow-up is an important part of making sure patients return to the practice.
- ☐ **Not taking advantage of online opportunities.** With the rise of digital technology, and the vast number of consumers choosing their dentist based on online ads and social media, it is imperative you dedicate resources to your online presence.
- ☐ **Neglecting to create a comprehensive business plan.** A dental practice should have an effective business plan that includes projected expenses, break-even points, and general financial forecasts. Without this foundation, the practice will not be able to measure whether their efforts are succeeding or failing. Don't forget the one page most people leave out...the page about who is going to buy your practice(s) in the future.

Best Practices in Growing from One Practice to Multiple Locations

- ☐ Research local markets and identify areas with potential growth, considering local competition, population density, median income, and community health initiatives.
- ☐ Develop a plan outlining the initiation of new locations while maintaining a strong presence in the existing location.
- ☐ Locate suitable real estate properties—existing practices vs. de novo (new construction)
- ☐ Utilize a dental office design firm
- ☐ Create an effective business plan with all financial forecasts
- ☐ Form a comprehensive communication plan to keep existing and new locations apprised of developments, changes, or updates
- ☐ Develop brand identity including professional website with prominent contact information, leads capture opt-in box, and social media presence
- ☐ Implement a customer relationship management system (CRM) or expand existing. Be thinking of creating a centralized CRM function for multiple practices
- ☐ Invest in marketing activities including social media, ads online and offline, partnering with other businesses and charities, or sponsorships of local events
- ☐ Recruit experienced team members—opportunity to promote existing team members to support opening team of next location
- ☐ Establish a referral system encouraging existing patients to refer their friends and family who live near the new practice location.
- ☐ Implement incentive programs for team members, such as bonuses and rewards to boost employee retention
- ☐ Ensure compliance with healthcare regulations at new locations
- ☐ Monitor progress in areas like patient satisfaction, employee retention, and financial performance at new locations
- ☐ Invest in state-of-the-art technology

Most Important Success Factors in Growing a Profitable Dental Practice

Profit Formula

Patient Visits X Production Amount per Visit X Collection% -- Overhead = Profits
The linchpins for maximizing profits are Patient Visits and Production Amount. Just a 10% gain in each produces a 20% increase to Profits. According to the ADA, and two research firms, the median overhead for a $1M practice is between 61.9% and 74.62%.

Hygiene Production
A well-trained team of hygienists are the foundation of your success with securing patient appointments for preventative services.

Become an Effective Leader
Lasting success in growing any dental practice requires the owner to navigate the role of manager and leader. Leaders build teams, systems, and businesses that grow and profit.

Same-Day Dentistry
Production increases with fewer cancellations when you are able to provide the convenience and efficiency of same-day dentistry.

Stay True to Your Goals
Stick to your business plan goals and objectives. Do not waiver. This is as important as a rudder to a ship to stay on track, maximize efficiency, productivity, and profitability.

Treatment Conversation Conversions (case acceptance)
Mastering the art and science of treatment conversations from language, scripting, process, and patient experience may turn out to be one of your biggest contributors to growth and profitability.

Roles and Responsibilities
When every team member fully understands their role and responsibilities and how they contribute to the success of the practice, everyone wins. Implementing Behavior Standards is another world-class best practice to achieve excellence.

Create Effective Efficient Systems
A true system includes 1) definition of success and why it matters; 2) flow diagram or process chart; 3) language and scripting; 4) follow-up; 5) clear metrics to measure.

Reducing Cancellations
Leveraging technology, systems, proper training, and offering same-day dentistry you can achieve appointment show-up rates of 96%+.

Wow Patient Experience
We are in the people business and creating magical experiences for our patients is critical to our success in so many ways—return patients, referrals, case acceptance, patient satisfaction, and profitability.

The 10 Performance Metrics Every Successful Dentist Entrepreneur Tracks

- ☐ New Patient Conversion Rate—inquiry to appointment
- ☐ Production Per Visit & Per Associate
- ☐ Gross & Net Production
- ☐ Cancellations %
- ☐ Treatment Acceptance Rate
- ☐ Collection Ratio—from billed to collected %
- ☐ Accounts Receivable—days to collect
- ☐ Overhead Costs
- ☐ Online Reviews and Patient Satisfaction
- ☐ Patient Retention

Seven Best Practices to Pre-Collect Funds from Patients Prior to Procedures

- ☐ **Offer Payment Plans**
  Provide patients with the option to pay in installments, e.g., third-party financing, allowing them to plan and budget their implant surgery in advance.

- ☐ **Make It Easy to Pay**
  Accept multiple forms of payments such as credit cards, checks, and digital wallets (Apple Pay, Google Pay, Venmo, Paypal, Square).

- ☐ **Automate Reminders**
  Send appointment reminders via email and text to patients prior to their visit with a link to pay outstanding balances electronically.

- ☐ **Educate Your Staff**
  Train your staff on the importance of pre-collecting payments and how it can help ensure all bills are paid in a timely manner.

- ☐ **Offer Incentives**
  Offering incentives for prepayment may encourage patients to pay for their treatments in advance.

- ☐ **Follow Up with Patients**
  Check in with patients by phone in a live conversation a few days before their scheduled appointment to ensure they have made payment arrangements and that bills are paid in full.

- ☐ **Appointment Check-in**
  Upon a patient's arrival for their appointment collect any payments before their appointment starts, rather than waiting until after the appointment. This contributes to a better patient experience as well.

There's No Standing Still

How to Grow a Profitable Dental Practice
Focusing on You,
Your People and Your Patients

Personal Action Guide

Dr. Sean Mohtashami

Made in the USA
Monee, IL
05 November 2026

67384081R00070